A ROMANTIC GUIDE TO HANDFASTING

Anna Franklin (England) has been a witch for 30 years, and a Pagan in her heart for all her life. She has conducted many rituals, handfastings, and sabbat rites. She is the author of *Midsummer, The Fairy Ring,* and *The Sacred Circle Tarot* as well as sixteen other books on witchcraft, folklore, and Paganism. She is the coauthor, with Paul Mason, of *Lammas.*

A

ROMANTIC

GUIDE TO

HANDFASTING

Rituals, Recipes
& Lore

Anna Franklin

Llewellyn Publications
Saint Paul, Minnesota

First Edition
First Printing, 2004

Cover background © by Brand X Pictures, cover flower image © by PhotoDisc
Cover design by Kevin R. Brown
Edited by Andrea Neff

Franklin, Anna.
  A romantic guide to handfasting : rituals, recipes & lore / Anna Franklin.—1st ed.
    p.   cm.
  Includes index.
  ISBN 0-7387-0668-X
   1. Marriage customs and rites. 2. Marriage—Religious aspects—Neopaganism.
  3. Marriage—Religious aspects—Goddess religion.   I. Title.

  GT2960.F73 2004
  392.5—dc22   2004054105

Llewellyn Publications
A Division of Llewellyn Worldwide, Ltd.
P.O. Box 64383, Dept. 0-7387-0668-X
St. Paul, MN 55164-0383, U.S.A.
www.llewellyn.com

Printed in the United States of America

Other Works by Anna Franklin

Hearth Witch
(Lear Books, 2004)

Watercolor Fairies
with David Riche
(Quarto, 2004)

The Illustrated Encyclopaedia of Fairies
with Paul Mason and Helen Field, illustrators
(Tiger, 2004; Chrysalis, 2002)

The Celtic Animal Oracle
(Chrysalis, 2003)

The Oracle of the Goddess
(Chrysalis, 2003)

The Fairy Ring: An Oracle of the Fairy Folk
with Paul Mason, illustrator
(Llewellyn Publications, 2002)

Midsummer
(Llewellyn Publications, 2002)

Real Wicca for Teenagers
(Capall Bann, 2002)

Lammas
with Paul Mason, coauthor
(Llewellyn Publications, 2001)

Fairy Lore
with Paul Mason, illustrator
(Capall Bann, 2000)

Magical Incenses and Oils
(Capall Bann, 2000)

The Wellspring
with Pamela Harvey and Helen Field
(Capall Bann, 2000)

Pagan Feasts
(Capall Bann, 1999)

Familiars
(Capall Bann, 1998)

Personal Power
(Capall Bann, 1998)

The Sacred Circle Tarot: A Celtic Pagan Journey
with Paul Mason, illustrator
(Llewellyn Publications, 1998)

Herb Craft
with Sue Lavender
(Capall Bann, 1997)

Forthcoming Works by Anna Franklin

Spellcaster
with Elen Hawke, et al.
(Llewellyn Publications, 2005)

Priest and Priestess
(Lear Books, 2005)

Shamanic Wicce
with Kathy Cocks
(Lear Books, 2005)

Working With Fairies
(Career Press, 2005)

Dedication

For lovers everywhere.

Acknowledgments

Thanks to everyone at Llewellyn for supporting this project, particularly Kevin R. Brown for his lovely cover design, and Andrea Neff for her painstaking and insightful editing skills. Thanks to Wade White for his invaluable help on gay deities.

Contents

INTRODUCTION

A handfasting is a Pagan wedding, usually the union of two individuals, perhaps two members of a coven or solo practitioners, who meet and fall in love. It is the marriage rite used today by many Pagans, druids, and Wiccans. During the ceremony, the couple declare their love and commitment to each other, and promise that they will live together for a year and a day or "for as long as love shall last," in the words of one ritual. At the end of that time, they may renew their vows, make a more permanent commitment and a legal marriage, or go their separate ways. In an age when, for whatever reason, many relationships do not last a lifetime and divorce is commonplace, a handfasting is perhaps a sensible option.

It might seem to be a very modern concept, but the idea of a trial marriage—usually for a year and a day—is very old. In the south of England, in Dorset, there is a cliff called Handfast Point where, presumably, many such unions were made. The ancient and medieval Irish would undertake trial marriages, clasping hands through a holed stone. If the couple got on, they would make more permanent vows; if not, they would go back to the stone, and each walk off in a different direction. Some think that this is where the term handfasting originated;

others think it may have come from the custom of shaking hands over a contract. Then too, in some cultures, the hands of the bride and groom are bound together, and many Pagans adopt this practice as part of the handfasting ceremony.

Many Pagans think that it is very important for them to be able to declare their commitment to each other in a ritual that expresses their own beliefs, feeling that a secular ceremony is not as fulfilling and meaningful as a declaration of love before their gods and their peers. The vows are usually written by the couple themselves to express their own needs and emotions. The handfasting is generally celebrated inside a magic circle, something that Pagans believe to exist "between the worlds," i.e., neither wholly in the mundane world of humankind nor wholly in the Otherworld of gods and spirits, but partly in both. What happens in the circle affects not only this world, but also the Otherworld. The circle stands at the intersection of the worlds for the time it is invoked. For a brief moment it becomes the center of the universe, and what happens within it during the handfasting ceremony reenacts the great cosmic theme of the love of the Goddess and the God. Their eternal romance is recreated and renewed by every human pair of lovers. They enter the circle as two separate people, and emerge as a couple. This is a life-changing event, and one of the most important rites of passage in life's journey.

The handfasting vows are believed, literally, to be taken before the gods, and are therefore very solemn and binding. Members of the coven or druidic grove act as witnesses, sometimes with friends and family present (if they would like to be), with the ritual presided over by a priest or priestess, druid, clan chieftain, or shaman. The couple exchange vows, promising to love and honor each other, and may give each other rings, have their hands loosely tied with colored cords or ribbons, jump over the cauldron or broomstick, and share wine together. Afterward there are the usual congratulations, the throwing of confetti or rice, posing for photographs, and a picnic or party. The handfasting may be followed by a civil wedding.

At the time of writing, handfasting has no legal validity in most states of the United States or in Britain and other parts of the world. Some Pagans hope that this will change with time as the Pagan religion becomes more accepted by the wider world. However, some more traditional Pagans think that this kind of trial marriage only needs to be recognized by family and clan, and that giving it a legal status would negate the purpose of a trial marriage. Over the years, the fundamental idea of the handfasting has changed among some Pagan groups, and the initial idea of a trial marriage of a year and a day has given way to the permanent vows of a conventional marriage.

Please note that the handfasting rite may be used by heterosexual couples or by partners of the same sex. It may even be adapted to encompass group marriages. The ideas in this book are only a starting point for your ceremony. Feel free to modify and change them according to your needs, and to write your own rituals and vows. The day is yours, so you can shape it the way you want.

Chapter 1

THE HISTORICAL BACKGROUND

Contrary to popular belief, marriages in the old days did not always take place with the benefit of clergy. Oftentimes only the rich could afford a church ceremony (which took place in the porch of the church, not inside), and in any case, in some areas, priests were thin on the ground, and one could not be found to conduct every marriage. In most parts of Europe, a declaration before witnesses was enough to constitute a legal marriage recognized by Roman Catholic Canon law. Even children were married in this manner, with the consummation sometimes taking place years later. It wasn't until 1563 that the Council of Trent changed the law, and a priest and marriage ceremony were required to constitute a valid marriage in Catholic countries.

Roman Common-Law Marriages

The ancient Romans could celebrate marriage *ex usu,* by which, if a woman, with the consent of her parents or guardians, lived with a man for a year without being absent for three nights, she became his legal wife. This custom was obsolete in Roman law by the time of the Republic.

English Handfastings

The term handfasting originates in the Anglo-Saxon word *handfæs-tung,* which meant the shaking of hands to seal a contract. A similar word exists in German and Danish. Among other things, it was applied to the act of betrothal in both England and Scotland. This betrothal itself was called, in Anglo-Saxon, a *beweddung,* because the future husband was called upon to make a down payment, or *wed,* against the bride price of his lady. (This is the origin of our term *wedding.*) The contract was sealed with a handshake, or handfæstung.

Irish Handfastings

In ancient Ireland, Teltown Marriages were temporary unions entered into at Lughnasa, the festival celebrated at the beginning of August. At Larganeeny (*Lag an Aonaigh,* "the hollow of the fair"), there was an oral tradition, recorded in the nineteenth century, that a form of marriage was held there in Pagan times. According to this legend, a number of young men would go to the north side of a high wall, while a number of young women went to the south side. A woman would then put her hand through a hole in the wall, and a man would take it, guided in his choice only by the appearance of the hand. The two who had thus joined hands by blind chance were then obliged to live together for a year and a day. At the end of that time they appeared together at the Rath (Fort) of Teltown, and if they were not satisfied, they obtained a deed of separation and were entitled to go to Larganeeny again to get a new partner. If they were satisfied, a longer-term arrangement was entered into.

One of the largest Lughnasa fairs was held at Kirkwall in the Orkney Islands off the coast of Scotland. The fair lasted eleven days, and taking a sexual partner for its duration was a common practice. Such couples were known as "Lammas brothers and sisters." For couples thinking of a slightly longer-term commitment, this was a traditional time for handfasting. Couples would join hands through a holed stone, such as the ancient Stone of Odin at Stenness, and plight their troth for a year and a day. Many such temporary unions became permanent arrangements. The handfasting ritual was just one of the forms of marriages permitted under the ancient Brehon law. The same law declared how the property would be divided if the couple split up, and how any children of the marriage would be cared for.

It wasn't until the middle of the nineteenth century that the registration of marriages was required by the government in Ireland.

Scottish Handfastings

In Scotland, the civil authorities recognized marriages constituted in the old style—consent to marry followed by intercourse at some later date—though the Scottish Church did not. Such marriages were legal until 1940. As a result, many English couples whose parents objected to their marriages crossed to the Scottish border town of Gretna Green where they could perform their own handfastings before witnesses. In Scotland, the term handfasting, or *handfisting,* meant the shaking of hands to seal a contract. This might be a contract of employment or a betrothal.

In 1820, the famous Scottish novelist Sir Walter Scott wrote of handfasting as a trial marriage in *The Monastery:*

> When we are handfasted, as we term it, we are man and wife for a year and a day; that space gone by, each may choose another mate, or, at their pleasure, may call the priest to marry them for life; and this we call handfasting.

The practice was also mentioned by Thomas Pennant, recounting his tour of Scotland in 1772:

> Among the various customs now obsolete the most curious was that of handfisting, in use about a century past. In the upper part of Eskdale . . . there was an annual fair where multitudes of each sex repaired. The unmarried looked out for mates,

made their engagements by joining hands, or by handfisting, went off in pairs, cohabited until the next annual return of the fair, appeared there again and then were at liberty to declare their approbation or dislike of each other. If each party continued constant, the handfisting was renewed for life.[1]

This account was confirmed in *The Old Statistical Account of Scotland*:

> At that fair [in Eskdale], it was the custom for the unmarried persons of both sexes to choose a companion, according to their liking, with whom they were to live till that time next year. This was called hand-fasting, or hand in fist. If they were pleased with each other at that time, then they continued together for life; if not, they separated, and were free to make another choice as at the first. The fruit of their connexion (if there were any) was always attached to the disaffected person. In later times . . . a priest . . . came from time to time to confirm the marriages.[2]

Welsh Broom-Jumping Weddings

There was a custom of jumping the broom as a declaration of marriage in both Wales and England. As a child I remember an old lady saying that a couple were "living over the brush," meaning that they were living together without being legally married, but had a common-law relationship obtained by jumping over a broom. In Wales, this was called the *priodas coes ysgub,* or broom-stick wedding.[3]

In Wales, a broom was placed on the doorstep with its handle leaning on the door frame, and the couple had to jump over it in front of witnesses. The couple were free to part within the first year, and simply had to jump over the broom again. If a child had been born, the man was obliged to support it. In Caernarvonshire, the practice was overseen by the oldest man in the village, and the broom was constructed of oak branches and called *ysgub dderwydd,* or "druid's besom," indicating that the custom may have been very old indeed, dating back to the time of the druids.

---

1. Thomas Pennant, *Tour of Scotland* (London, 1790).

2. *The Old Statistical Account of Scotland* (1791–99).

3. T. Gwynn Jones, *Welsh Folklore and Folk-Custom* (London: Methuen & Co., Ltd., 1930).

Chapter 2

ORGANIZING YOUR HANDFASTING

*W*hen you and your partner decide to become handfasted, there are a number of things to consider. Below is a checklist for organizing a handfasting ceremony, and a few things to think about along the way. Each point will be covered in greater detail later in the book.

- Firstly (and very importantly), decide how much money you have to spend on the handfasting, and budget accordingly.
- Determine the date: you might like to take into account the phases of the moon, "lucky" days, and so on.
- Decide on the style or theme of wedding (plain Pagan, Greek, Celtic, formal Wiccan, medieval, etc.).
- Draw up the guest list: decide on whom you want to be present at the handfasting, whether you want to invite just your coven or your non-Pagan friends and relatives too.
- Choose the site for the ceremony (indoors or outdoors). Make your booking or get any relevant permissions.

- Decide on the costumes or robes and who will wear them, and who will be responsible for paying for and supplying them.

- Who will officiate? A nominated celebrant should usually be in charge. This might be your high priest or priestess, druid, shaman, clan leader, or friend. You might need to request a priest and priestess from a Pagan organization (see appendix 5).

- Decide on the ritual and talk this over with the celebrant.

- Come to a decision on the type of commitment you wish to make to each other, whether it is for a year and a day or for longer.

- Write your vows.

- Choose which gods and goddesses you want to call on to bless the ceremony. Don't mix traditions or pantheons.

- Do you want to include the jumping of the broom or cauldron? Decide on any customs you want to be part of the event, and where they will fit into the ceremony.

- Settle on an order of service, write it down, and let everyone who will be attending have a copy.

- If you are having a legal civil ceremony before or afterward, this will need to be coordinated with the ritual. Check out the legalities of handfasting in your area.

- Make sure that you let your guests know what will be happening, what they will need to bring, and what they will be expected to do.

- Organize the flowers, garlands, chaplets, and bouquets.

- Make the incense and anointing oils (if used), get a friend to make them, or purchase them if necessary.

- You might like to give the guests a small gift, such as a little posy or lucky charm.

- If you want to exchange rings, you will need to buy these or have them made. Do you want them inscribed?

- Do you want music at the handfasting or at the party afterward? You might like to use live music suitable to the theme, or allow the coven bards and minstrels to perform. Alternatively, if you use recorded music, you will need to organize a sound system to play this on.

- You might like to have a handfasting certificate, signed by the celebrant. Some priests and priestesses supply these, or you could design one on a computer, print it, and ask the celebrant to sign it.

- Buy or make the cords that you will use to bind the hands.

- Decide on how you will decorate the circle, where you will place the altar and how you will dress it, and so on.

- Determine whether you want an after-ritual party or picnic and book the venue.

- Organize the catering.

- Design and send your invitations, telling people the time, date, venue, and describing what they might need to wear or bring.

- How will you and the guests get to the venue? Do you need to arrange transportation for everyone?

- Would you like photographs of the event? You could employ a photographer, or just encourage friends to take pictures and let you have copies.

- Will you be going on a honeymoon afterward? This needs to be booked and transportation arranged.

- Don't forget to send thank-you notes to everyone who helped you achieve your perfect handfasting.

Budgeting for the Handfasting

You can see from this checklist that there will be a number of expenses incurred in organizing a handfasting. The event can be as simple or as lavish as you wish or can afford. You could have a beautiful, simple ritual attended by friends and relatives and a picnic afterward. Or you could have everyone dressed in medieval costume serenaded by minstrels and followed by a banquet, but this will be expensive! Take into account the cost of flowers, food, transportation, clothes, rings, cords, incense, entertainment, and so on. If you are not careful, you might be horrified by a big bill when you get back from your honeymoon, which would not be a good start to married life!

The Celebrant

Though you and your partner can simply exchange vows in front of witnesses, it is more usual to have a celebrant preside over the ritual. If you belong to a coven, this might be your high priestess or high priest, or both acting together. If you belong to a druid grove, the chief druid will probably be happy to perform the ceremony. Alternatively, you might ask the head of your Pagan clan, the local shaman, or simply a Pagan friend whom you trust. If necessary, you could apply to a Pagan organization, such as the Pagan Federation, to put you in touch with a priest or priestess to help you. Some useful addresses can be found in appendix 5.

The Groomsman

It is the custom for the groom to be attended by a groomsman. Long ago, it was the practice among some Germanic tribes to kidnap women from a nearby village to marry. Rather than undertake the enterprise alone, a man would take his best friend along to help him. This is probably the origin of the "best man" role. He was also called the *bridesman* or *brideknight,* and in more troubled times, it was part of his duty to safeguard the wedding party. One of the reasons the bride stands to the left of the groom is so that his sword arm is free to protect her.

The Bridesmaid

The bride is attended by a married woman, called the *matron of honor,* and by young unmarried girls called *bridesmaids.* In the past, they all dressed the same and were veiled, and the groom was faced with the challenge of having to pick out his bride from the throng. As recently as Victorian times, the bridesmaids wore veils and dressed in white, like the bride.

Another reason the bridesmaids dressed like the bride was to confuse evil spirits who might try to spoil the wedding. This way, they wouldn't know who to choose!

Family and Friends

Along with your coven or grove, it is natural to want to share your special day with family and friends, even if they are not Pagan. If you think they would be happy to attend, invite them along, but do not insist. Not everyone is yet comfortable with attending a Pagan ceremony. To reassure them, you should let them know everything that will happen on the day, and explain the reasons behind each ritual act. They may like to watch from outside the circle, or if your celebrant is okay with the idea, they might enjoy the experience of being part of the circle.

The Venue

Ideally, every Pagan would like to be married outdoors in some beautiful spot, preferably an ancient stone circle. However, this is not possible in all cases, and you could consider woods, the seashore, or secluded parkland. Whenever you hold a ritual outside, you need to make sure that the location is private and that you obtain any relevant permissions.

Maybe you would rather not risk the weather (depending on where you live) and would like to be handfasted at home or, if you do not have the space, in a rented hall, hotel, or community center. Again, be sure that the proprietors are comfortable with what you are going to do and know what to expect.

If at all possible, decorate the site with greenery, flowers, and colored ribbons. You might like to outline the circle with flowers or crystals on this occasion. If the site permits, you could follow the medieval custom of strewing the floor with scented herbs: rosemary for constancy, lemon balm for joy, mint for clarity, and so on.

The Reception

The reception may take place at the same site as the handfasting, or the party might adjourn to a hall or hotel after an outdoor handfasting. If possible, decorate the hall with garlands of greenery, ivy, and flowers. Wild flowers are particularly charming and have more significance than bought flowers—they are cheaper too! Include decorations associated with fertility and abundance, including wheat, fruit, and nuts. These can be made into table decorations and centerpieces.

Sweets symbolize sweetness in the relationship, and are traditional in many cultures. They can be placed in dishes at intervals along the buffet, or gilded and scattered artistically along the tables. Decorate the place settings or buffet with sprigs of herbs, and twine some into the napkin rings.

Ask the owners or managers of the hotel or hall where the reception will take place if you can erect an altar. Place them on a decorated cloth and arrange offerings of flowers and fruit before them. You might make paper hangings of suns, moons, stars, and pentacles.

For the duration of the feast, the bride and groom may be placed on chairs or thrones of honor, beneath a canopy or bridal arch of flowers. Elizabethan couples sat under a *kissing knot,* a wreath of herbs decorated with trailing ribbons, which was hung over them.

The Commitment

As I said in the introduction, the traditional handfasting is a trial marriage, which may then be renewed with a more permanent commitment or abandoned. Modern Pagans often substitute the handfasting ceremony for a more conventional marriage ceremony, making the lifelong vows of marriage.

You need to consider the kind of vows that you will make to your beloved, whether you will enter into the trial marriage of handfasting or make a more permanent commitment. The traditional handfasting promises include:

> *I give myself to [name] for a year and a day.*

or

> *I give myself to [name] for thirteen moons.*

If you make this promise, you must see it through for one year. It is a solemn vow before the gods. If you decide to go your separate ways after a year, you might simply part, or have a formal handparting.

You might not even want to make a time commitment at all, but say:

> *For as long as love shall last.*

or

> *While we both shall love.*

This gives you the option to part before the year is up, or to stay together for a year, five years, twenty years, or the rest of your lives. If you decide to part, you might choose to have a handparting ceremony.

If, after a year or more, you want to make a more permanent commitment, you might perform the handfasting again, saying something like this:

> *While love shall last.*

Or, if you think you really have found your soul mate, you might make a lifetime declaration such as this:

> *For this lifetime.*

or

> *Until we are parted by death.*

Once again, remember that you are making a solemn vow before the gods. I would urge you to think very carefully indeed before undertaking it. Though many people take vows and oaths lightly in today's society and think nothing of breaking them, this is not the way of the Pagan, whose oath is made before the Old Gods and is unbreakable, a matter of honor. If you make a solemn vow before the gods and break it, there will be a heavy karmic price to pay, so think carefully before making any promise. A handparting is not the same as a divorce, and does not negate your oath. An oath that you make thinking that you can take it back later is not an oath, and the gods see into your heart, even if no one else does.

Please do not even consider the entirely modern practice of soul binding, which binds the couple's souls together throughout all future incarnations as part of the rite. I believe this practice to be highly dangerous and very wrong. I have known people bound in this way to handpart after a year and a day, finding that their love was merely physical attraction and not the deep love of the *anam cara,* or "soul friend." But, calamitously, because of their soul binding, they are doomed to go throughout life after life, meeting, mating, and parting in disappointment. If you are truly twin souls, then you will meet time after time anyway, perhaps not in every incarnation, but as you are meant to for your individual developments.

Chapter 3

THE RITUALS

Handfastings are conducted in a circle, itself an important Pagan symbol. It has no beginning and no end. It is eternal. When the magician casts a circle, he or she creates a space apart from ordinary life: an interface between the mundane plane of waking consciousness and the realm of the gods and spirits, which we might call the Otherworld. When the magician enters the circle, he or she leaves the ordinary world behind and enters a domain apart: a realm of sacred space and time. When the magic circle is properly built, cast, and invoked, it becomes the universe in microcosm; i.e., it creates in miniature the entire cosmos. The complete circle represents its oneness, while the divisions of the circle stand for the passing of time and the seasons, the space in which the universe exists, and the substances and energies of which it is made. Whatever the magician performs within this magical microcosm will be reflected in the macrocosm. In other words, each ritual act will be made manifest in the macrocosm, whether it is the reenactment of a seasonal myth or the love of two people, which will echo throughout the universe.

The Perfect Circle

The circle is a universal emblem of wholeness and completion. It symbolizes continuity, eternity, completion, and spacelessness: the absence of time and space. As it represents what is complete and unbroken, it also stands for everlasting love. Mark the perimeter of the circle with flowers, crystals, shells, or pink, white, or red candles. You can also scatter petals around the circle after it has been ritually swept.

The circle can be divided: halved, quartered, separated into degrees, and so on. However, far from symbolizing dissolution and imperfection, when these fractions are contained within the circle, they represent the balance and harmony of such divisions. Think of the famous yin-yang symbol, which represents the reconciliation of opposites within the whole. Within the circle, opposites (such as day and night, summer and winter) are united. Within the circle, their division is not absolute, but each gives rise to the other, reconciled in the circle of unity, just as the two halves of a couple make up the whole.

The Cardinal Points

The four main compass points of the circle are called the *cardinal points*. When the magic circle is drawn, it is aligned to the cardinal points of the compass—north, south, east, and west. This is not merely symbolic; the east of the circle should be aligned with the real east, and so on. The flow of earth power is north to south. The North Star stands at the north of the circle. The Celts called it *Caer Arianrhod,* the Spiral Castle. It was the entrance to the Otherworld, and the place of death and rebirth. The circle must be orientated with the energies of the cosmos.

When the circle is cast by the magician, each direction is invoked in turn and the circle is thus spatially orientated. This operation is often called the *summoning* or *invocation of the Watchtowers*.

North

The north is the point of the circle associated with the winter solstice (Yule), cold, darkness, midnight, starlight, regeneration, rebirth, and life through death, since it is at the winter solstice that the sun is reborn. The sun then gains strength and grows stronger up until the summer solstice. The north is associated with the element of earth. Place a dish of salt, soil, pebbles, or a large stone or crystal in the north.

East

The east is the point of the circle associated with the spring equinox. The east is associated with sunrise, dawn, and gestation, the beginning of growth; a time of green youth. It is connected with the element of air. In a stone circle oriented to the vernal equinox, the sun will rise directly in the east, over the east stone at the equinox. Place a dish of incense or a feather in the east.

South

The south is the point of the circle associated with the summer solstice, with the zenith of the sun's strength, midday, ripeness, flowering, maturity, and the prime of life. It is connected with the element of fire. Place a lighted candle in the south.

West

The west is the point of the circle associated with the autumn equinox and the completion of the harvest, with twilight, sunset, completion, and decline. It is linked with the element of water. Place a dish or cup of water in the west. You could float some rose petals on the surface of the water.

The Directions of Above and Below

The celestial realms of above and the underworld realm of below stand above and below the circle, and their powers are called upon, drawn through the axis of the circle as the first step of its casting. Thus the invoked circle is not a two-dimensional object, but a sphere, extending below ground and above, in which the magician operates.

The Center of the Circle

The central point represents the place where all powers meet, where all times and places are one. For the Celts it was the Spiral Castle, a place of regeneration and rebirth. The axis through the center links all the realms and times. The cardinal points are often called the *quarters*, which are further associated with the four elements. These are invoked when the circle is cast so that the ring becomes a place of balanced energies.

The four directions (the four Royal Roads of Power) coming from the cardinal points meet at the center of the circle. This point becomes the *axis mundi,* the center of all things where all times and places are one, from which all things are accessible. It may be symbolized by the pillar, the shaman's ladder, the world tree, or the cauldron of renewal.

The Altar

Set up the altar in the northern quarter of the circle. A low table or chest can be employed. Cover it with a pink or red cloth and scatter it with rose petals. Place three pink candles (for love) in holders on the altar, or use red (for passion) or green (for the heart chakra and unconditional love). Place a dish of salt and a dish of water near the front of the altar. You will also need a knife that you keep for ritual purposes, which some people call an *athame.* You can decorate the altar with flowers, greenery, fruit, nuts, heart shapes, and so on. The chalice should be filled with red wine, or you could go all out and fill it with champagne. Place the book of rituals where you can see it. You will also need the silken cords for binding, the rings, and equipment for any other customs you wish to include.

Casting the Circle

What I present here is only one method of casting a circle. There are many others, but the principle of establishing a boundary between the mundane world and a sacred space where ritual acts are carried out remains the same.

Place a candle in each of the quarters, choosing colors that resonate with the vibration of that quarter: green for the north (earth), yellow for the east (air), red for the south (fire), and blue for the west (water). If you can't get these, you can use white candles, but the more you reinforce the imagery, the more it helps your visualization. Check that you have everything you need within the circle (remember the matches!) before you start, as once the circle is cast, you will not be able to leave to get anything.

Sweep the circle with the broom. If you'd like, you can then scatter the circle with flower petals.

Begin by lighting the incense. The first act that must be performed is to establish the boundaries of the circle. Take the knife and draw the circle around the room, beginning in the north. Remember that wherever the point of the knife draws will be the edge of the circle. Include all the things and people you wish to be within the circle. Then say:

> *I conjure thee, O circle of power, that thou mayest be a meeting place of love and joy and truth, a boundary between the world of men and the realms of the Otherworld, containing the power that we shall raise within thee, but a shield and protection against our enemies, both visible and invisible.*

Take the knife and place the tip in the bowl of salt, saying:

> *Be this salt dedicated to the Lord and Lady [or whatever deities you call upon], to keep us from evil and protect us in this time.*

Take the knife again and place the tip in the bowl of water, saying:

> *Be this water dedicated to the Lord and Lady, to keep us from*
> *peril and to purify this place.*

Pour the water into the salt and mix them together. Sprinkle clockwise (deosil) around the circle, saying:

> *May we cast from us all evil and darkness, viciousness and mal-*
> *ice. May we become that which we must be before the Lord and Lady,*
> *seeking ill to no one. May we be clean within and without so that we*
> *are acceptable before them.*

Finish by sprinkling each person in turn.

Next, connect the circle to all three realms. Take the knife and stand in the center of the circle. Point it above and say:

> *Powers of the worlds above, I do summon, stir, and call you up to*
> *guard our circle and to witness our rites.*

Bring the knife down in a straight line and point it downward. Say:

> *Powers of the worlds below, I do summon, stir, and call you up to*
> *guard our circle and to witness our rites.*

The Watchtowers are then invoked. Take the knife and begin in the north. The casting of the circle is always begun in the north as this is the place of power that flows from north to south, so the gateway to this power is opened first. Many people do not begin the invocations until reaching the east, as this is the direction of vocalization. Draw a pentacle in the east and say:

> *O mighty powers of the east, I do summon, stir, and call you up to*
> *guard our circle and to witness our rites.*

Repeat this in the south, west, and north.

Return to the altar and consecrate the altar candles with these words:

I consecrate these candles that they shall represent light and knowledge within this circle.

Light the altar candles and take one around to light all the quarter candles. If you wish, you can carry the dish of incense around the circle.

The work of the ritual is now performed.

Dissolving the Circle

When all ritual work is finished, it is time to dissolve the circle. Take the knife and cut through the boundary of the circle near the east and say:

Mighty powers of the east, thank you for guarding our circle and for witnessing our rites. I bless you in the name of the Lord and the Lady [or whatever deities you call upon].

Repeat in the other three directions. Cut through the center of the circle and thank the powers of above and below.

Put out the candles and dismantle the temple.

Handfasting Rituals

The rituals in this book are included to give you some basic outlines for the ceremony and a few ideas to start you off. Remember that this is your special day, so you should tailor the ceremony to fit your needs. In particular, you should create your own vows, words that express your feelings; this will be more meaningful than anything I could write.

A Pagan Handfasting

The circle is laid out by the bridesmaids as a ring of flowers. In the north, which represents the element of earth and the physical realm, the bridesmaids place a dish of salt and bread. In the east, which represents the element of air and the mental realm, they place a feather and the dish of incense, lighting it. In the south, which represents the element of fire and the realm of will, they place a candle. In the west, which represents the realm of water and the emotions, they place a cup of water. They wait inside the circle.

The presiding priest or priestess enters the circle, followed by the bride and groom, the groomsman, and other guests. The groom stands to the left of the bride, with the best man slightly to one side and behind the groom, and the bridesmaid slightly to one side and behind the bride. Non-Pagan guests may prefer to watch from outside the circle, but this is up to the couple, priest/ess, and the guests themselves.

Priest/ess: *We are gathered here to witness the handfasting of [names of bride and groom] in the presence of the Old Gods and their brothers and sisters of the Old Ways. Be welcome, all those who come in perfect love and perfect trust. We call upon our lovely Lady of the Silver Moon and our gentle Lord of the Wildwood to be present here today to bless this act of love celebrated in their honor. So shall it be.*

All: *So shall it be.*

The priest/ess takes the couple and presents them to each of the quarters as follows:

Spirits of the north, you spirits of earth, know that [names of bride and groom] stand before you to seek the bond of handfasting. We ask you to witness this solemn rite. So shall it be.

All: *So shall it be.*

The priest/ess takes the couple and presents them to the east:

Spirits of the east, you spirits of air, know that [names of bride and groom] stand before you to seek the bond of handfasting. We ask you to witness this solemn rite. So shall it be.

All: *So shall it be.*

The priest/ess takes the couple and presents them to the south:

> *Spirits of the south, you spirits of fire, know that [names of bride and groom] stand before you to seek the bond of handfasting. We ask you to witness this solemn rite. So shall it be.*

All: *So shall it be.*

The priest/ess takes the couple and presents them to the west:

> *Spirits of the west, you spirits of water, know that [names of bride and groom] stand before you to seek the bond of handfasting. We ask you to witness this solemn rite. So shall it be.*

All: *So shall it be.*

The bride and groom are then led to the altar, where the rings (if used) are laid on the book of rituals. The priest/ess picks up the book and the rings and says:

> *The ring is the perfect circle, whole and unbroken. I bless these rings in the name of the God and Goddess that they symbolize the bond of true love between [names of bride and groom]. So shall it be.*

All: *So shall it be.*

Priest/ess [to the groom]: *[Name of groom], is it your wish that you shall become handfasted to [name of bride] before the Old Gods?*

Groom: *It is my wish to be handfasted to [name of bride] before the Old Gods and these witnesses.*

Priest/ess: *And do you pledge on your honor, and before the Old Gods and these witnesses, that you will ever strive for her happiness, placing it above your own from this day forward, for as long as love shall last between you?*

Groom: *I do so swear on my honor before the Old Gods and these witnesses that I will ever strive for [name of bride]'s happiness, placing it above my own from this day forward, for as long as love shall last between us.*

Priest/ess: *Then place your ring on her finger. [The groom does so.]*

Priest/ess [to the bride]: *[Name of bride], is it your wish that you shall become handfasted to [name of groom] before the Old Gods?*

Bride: *It is my wish to be handfasted to [name of groom] before the Old Gods and these witnesses.*

Priest/ess: *And do you pledge on your honor, and before the Old Gods and these witnesses, that you will ever strive for his happiness, placing it above your own from this day forward, for as long as love shall last between you?*

Bride: *I do so swear on my honor before the Old Gods and these witnesses that I will ever strive for [name of groom]'s happiness, placing it above my own from this day forward, for as long as love shall last between us.*

Priest/ess: *Then place your ring on his finger. [The bride does so.]*

The priest/ess takes the cords and fastens the hands of the bride and groom together, saying:

> *You are bound together by the rite of handfasting in the eyes of the Old Gods and the Old Ways. Ever love and help one another as you have promised here today. May the God and Goddess bless you. So shall it be.*

All: *So shall it be.*

The priest/ess takes the couple and presents them to each of the quarters as follows:

> *Spirits of the north, you spirits of earth, know that [names of bride and groom] share the bond of handfasting. Bestow on them, we beseech you, your gifts of plenty, good health, and fertility so that they shall always be happy together. So shall it be.*

All: *So shall it be.*

The couple eat some of the bread dipped in the salt.

The priest/ess takes the couple and presents them to the east:

Spirits of the east, you spirits of air, know that [names of bride and groom] share the bond of handfasting. Bestow on them, we beseech you, your gifts of knowledge, good communication, and inspiration so that they shall always be able to talk to each other and find pleasure in each other's company. So shall it be.

All: *So shall it be.*

The couple are purified with the incense and are given the feather.
The priest/ess takes the couple and presents them to the south:

Spirits of the south, you spirits of fire, know that [names of bride and groom] share the bond of handfasting. Bestow on them, we beseech you, your gifts of passion, vitality, and creativity so that their desire for each other shall not wane. So shall it be.

All: *So shall it be.*

The couple light the candle, holding the taper together.
The priest/ess takes the couple and presents them to the west:

Spirits of the west, you spirits of water, know that [names of bride and groom] share the bond of handfasting. Bestow on them, we beseech you, your gifts of friendship, support, and love. So shall it be.

All: *So shall it be.*

The couple both drink from the cup and are led back to the altar.

Priest/ess: *Let all of us now offer blessings and congratulations to [names of bride and groom].*

Everyone speaks any prepared or spontaneous blessings they have and showers the couple with flower petals. The broom is brought forward and the couple is encouraged to jump over it for luck.

Priest/ess: *As it has been since the beginning of time, and as it shall be till the end, two lovers have been joined together, and by this have been made stronger, happier, and greater than they were apart, and the simple fact that their love exists in the world benefits us all. This wondrous* *state is the gift of our gracious Lady and her own gentle Lord, whose love flows through all things, and whose passion we see reflected throughout the seasons, and which is the deepest mystery of our faith.*

The bridesmaids open the flower circle.

Priest/ess: *The circle is open but unbroken. What we have witnessed here today will remain in our hearts. We thank the spirits of north, south, east, and west for their presence. We thank our gracious Lord and Lady for their blessings. Blessings be on all. So shall it be.*

All: *So shall it be!*

This is the signal for the feast and games to begin.

A Wiccan Handfasting

Place three pink candles in holders on the altar. Place a dish of salt and a dish of water near the front of the altar, and a plate of bread or cakes and some wine in an open bottle or jug to one side. You will need a cup or goblet for drinking the wine and a pentacle of clay or copper. You will also need an athame (the witch's ritual knife).

Place a glass or clay cup on the altar. The couple will drink from this cup and then break it as a token that no other shall share what they have together. In addition, place the two rings on the book of rituals. Place flowers such as meadowsweet, apple blossom, violets, cherry blossom, and roses on the altar and about the circle, and wreath them into chaplets for the couple and their guests.

Cast the circle in the usual manner.

The priestess invokes the Goddess:

[Goddess name], I invoke and call upon thee, threefold goddess of the moon, queen of the moonlit sea, fairer than night and silver clad. Thee, I invoke, mother of the moon and calm waters. Let thy light fall upon us for thy hair is a pool of stars in the darkness. I call upon thee, widow of the waning moon whose children have left thee to sorrow. Guard us with learning and grant us a place in thy dark cloak of

understanding. Thee, I invoke. Descend, I beseech thee, and be with us now.

The priest invokes the God:

Lord of the heaven and power of the sun, lord of the hunt and forests, I invoke thee in thy secret name of [God name]. Come unto us and honor our circle, we beg of you. Mighty one, our Lord, all honor to thee, consort of the Goddess. Come, I call upon thee. Descend, I beseech thee, and be with us now.

The priest or the priestess states the purpose of the ritual:

Lord and Lady, God and Goddess, sacred pair who were with us before the dawn of time and shall be till its dusk, hear now the purpose of this ritual and witness it. Two of your secret children wish to share the bond of handfasting, declaring their love before thee and their brothers and sisters of the Craft.

Everyone joins in the circle dance and chant to raise power:

Thrice about the altar go
Once for Virgin pure as snow,
Once for Full Moon's soft sweet breath,
Once for Dark Moon, old as death,
Thrice about the altar spin
That the right shall well begin.

Priest: *Who among you seeks the bond of handfasting?*

Priestess: *Let them be named and brought forward.*

Groomsman: *[Groom's name] is the man.*

Bridesmaid: *[Bride's name] is the woman.*

Priestess [to groom]: *Are you [groom's name]?*

Groom: *I am.*

Priestess: And what is your desire?

Groom: To be handfasted to [bride's name] before the Lord and Lady and my brothers and sisters of the Craft.

Priest [to bride]: Are you [bride's name]?

Bride: I am.

Priest: And what is your desire?

Bride: To be handfasted to [groom's name] before the Lord and Lady and my brothers and sisters of the Craft.

Priestess [holds the coven sword or her athame aloft]: Aradia, Cernunnos [or whatever deity names your coven uses], here before you stand two of your secret people. Witness now what they have to declare [she places the sword or athame at the groom's chest]. Repeat after me:

"I, [groom's name], do come here of my own free will to seek the partnership of [bride's name]. I come with all honor, love, and sincerity, wishing only to become one with her whom I love. Always will I strive for [bride's name]'s happiness and welfare. Her life will I defend before my own. May this sword be plunged into my chest should I not be sincere in all that I declare. All this I swear before Cernunnos and Aradia. May they give me strength to keep my vows. So mote it be."

The priest repeats the procedure with the bride.

The couple are anointed with handfasting oil.

If rings are used, they are blessed by the priest and priestess at this point, in the name of the God and Goddess, and exchanged by the bride and groom, who now make their own vows.

A small cup of wine is brought forward.

Priestess: Drink your fill of the cup of love.

The cup is shared by the couple, which is then broken to denote that no other shall partake of what they have together. (Wrap the cup in a cloth to avoid dangerous flying shards, and have a small hammer ready to do the deed.)

The priest then binds their hands together with the cords, saying:

Know that you are bound for a year and a day in the eyes of the Gods and your brothers and sisters of the Craft. You shall return in thirteen moons to this place to renew your vows or go your separate ways. Know that this is a solemn vow, and you are one. Ever love, honor, and respect each other.

Cakes and wine are blessed and shared by everyone present. The priestess takes the wine and pours it into the chalice, saying:

Lord and Lady, I call upon thee to bless this wine, the blood of the earth pressed smooth. As we drink of thee, may we learn of the wisdom of the Goddess.

The wine is passed around clockwise. The priestess blesses the cakes:

Lord and Lady, I call upon thee to bless these cakes, the fruit of the womb of the Goddess without which we would not live. As we eat of thee, may we learn of the love of the Goddess.

The cakes are passed around.

When all is finished, the circle is dissolved. The priestess takes the knife and cuts through the boundary of the circle near the east and says:

Mighty powers of the east, thank you for guarding our circle and for witnessing our rites. I bless you in the name of the Lord and the Lady.

The priestess repeats this in the other three directions. She cuts through the center of the circle and thanks the powers of above and below. She does not dismiss the Lord and Lady, but thanks them:

Companions, we have met together this night to celebrate the handfasting of [groom's name], our brother, and [bride's name], our sister. Together we have worked for our purposes. The God and Goddess have witnessed our workings and only they will measure our purposes and our hearts. Together we have invoked for power to accomplish our working, but it is not for us to command those whom we worship. Nor is it for us to bid them be gone. We cannot dismiss them. I ask instead of the Lord and Lady that they be with us all our days, guiding our feet and lighting our paths. I ask that the Lord and Lady be with us in our lives and in our deaths, our true parents, even as we are their children. Let the circle be extinguished, but let us not forget the workings of this night. Let the candles be put out, but let us not forget what we have learned. Let the rite be ended now in the knowledge that we shall meet once more.

Before the Lord and Lady, Cernunnos and Aradia, God and Goddess, the rite is ended. Blessed Be.

The broomstick is brought forward and the couple are jokingly told that they must jump over it once for each child they wish to have. They are showered with rice, rose petals, meadowsweet, violets, wheat, and orange blossom.

Alternate Handfasting Ritual

Lay out a circle of crystals (ideally rose quartz). Cast the circle in the usual manner.

Priest: *We call upon the Lord, whom we worship, Angus Og, the young god of love who sparks desire. Be with us to witness the joining of [names of bride and groom] in the rite of handfasting.*

Priestess: *We call upon our Lady, the beautiful Aine, the goddess of love, white-fingered and sensual. Be with us to witness the joining of [names of bride and groom] in the rite of handfasting.*

Priest [to bride]: *Do you come here freely to seek the bond of handfasting with [name of groom]?*

Bride: *I do.*

Priestess [to groom]: Do you come here freely to seek the bond of hand-fasting with [name of bride]?

Groom: *I do.*

Priest: *Then before the gods and these witnesses, I bind you with this cord. It is the bond of love alone that joins you. Let it not be a restriction, but a loving sharing. Stand together, but not too close, for nothing thrives in the shadow of another. Listen to the music of the other's heart and appreciate it for its own beauty, and do not insist that your songs are the same. Let your love stand firm, like the mountains of the earth; let it sing like the wind in the trees and burn like the midsummer fires. Let your love flow like the tides of the sea, freely and always moving, soul to soul.*

The couple face each other and together they declare:

> *I offer you my body, that we may know pleasure together.*
> *I share with you my mind, that we may find wisdom together.*
> *I open my soul to you, that we may grow in spirit together.*
> *I offer you my heart, that we may love each other, wholly and*
> *   unselfishly.*
> *So mote it be.*

All: *So mote it be.*

The couple may exchange rings, gifts, and so on, if desired. The cakes and wine follow. The God and Goddess are thanked:

Priestess: *We thank you, Aine, for your presence here tonight. Give each of us your gift of love. Let each of us find the one who makes us more than we are, who brings us joy and happiness.*

Priest: *We thank you, Angus Og, for your presence here tonight. Give each of us your gift of love. Let each of us find it within our heart to love, to be the lover, to be loved.*

The circle is broken and the party begins.

The Great Rite

The Great Rite is a ritualized use of the sexual act (in actuality or, more usually, in a purely symbolic form) for magical purposes. It is the supreme joining of the male and female energies that shape the cosmos. Between two people, it is a deep connection whereby they open to each other physically and spiritually. Sexual union between two people can be a transcendent experience in which they touch the divine within.[1]

For Pagans, sex is not shameful or considered a taboo subject, but is a joyful celebration of being both human and part divine. The body is not something to be despised, but a great gift to be celebrated. Some witches from the newer traditions seem to think that the Great Rite is only used during initiation ceremonies, especially the third degree rite. This is not true. The American witch Starhawk called sex a Wiccan sacrament, an outward sign of inward grace, the "deep connection and recognition of the wholeness of another person . . . an exchange of energy, of subtle nourishment, between people."[2] It may be used to raise energy for magic, to conceive a magical child, or to consummate a handfasting. If it is to be symbolic, this takes the form of the athame, a masculine emblem, plunged into a chalice, which is a feminine image of the womb of the Goddess. This may be part of the handfasting ritual witnessed by the coven. If the Great Rite is to take place in actuality, this will be when everyone else has gone home, and the bride and groom are in the privacy of their chamber. The bedroom, too, can be a sacred temple.

Renewing the Vows

If the handfasting vow is for a year and a day, then the vows should be renewed after that time elapses. Another full ceremony can be held, with coven and witnesses present, or it may be a simple exchange of vows between the two people concerned. This time the couple may wish to make a more permanent arrangement or merely renew the arrangement for another year and a day. Otherwise, the handfasting lapses after thirteen moons and the two are free to go their separate ways with no recriminations. If both people agree, then a handparting ritual may be held to bring closure to the relationship.

1. Lira Silbury, *The Sacred Marriage* (Saint Paul, MN: Llewellyn Publications, 1994).

2. Starhawk, *The Spiral Dance* (1979; reprint, San Francisco, CA: HarperSanFrancisco, 1999).

Chapter 4

GODS AND GODDESSES

*W*iccans and most Pagans worship the Goddess and the God equally. The Goddess is the creator of the universe, giving birth to it from her cosmic womb. Every year, in the depths of winter, she gives birth to the God. As the spring blossoms, he grows to manhood and marries the Goddess in the heat of summer. With the declining days of autumn, he dies and is buried in the ground. But the earth is the womb of the Goddess, and from it, he is reborn once more. We call this the Eternal Return, and it is the oldest story in the world.

Together the Goddess and the God represent the whole of creation. He is male, she is female, he is the sun, she is the moon, he is the sky, and she is the earth nourished by his fertilizing rain. Pagans believe in a kind of cosmic harmony of opposing forces held in dynamic equilibrium, the male energy of the God and the female energy of the Goddess. The relationship of the God and Goddess is reflected in the love of human couples. Together the two opposites make one perfect whole, the two together capable of far more than each alone. Each person must recognize the divine part of themselves that is the Goddess or the God, and both partners must recognize it in each other. Only in this way can a sacred partnership be formed "in perfect love and perfect trust." Each partner honors the Goddess or the God within the other.

The Bride and the Goddess

During the sacred rite of handfasting, the bride represents the Goddess, and for that moment, she is the Goddess in her bridal aspect, her love uplifting and changing everyone present, but especially her bridegroom. The man recognizes the Goddess in his bride and approaches her with love and great respect. She is not his chattel, as in some Christian ceremonies, and she does not promise to obey him. They are equal partners in life. Together they are the balance of male and female, day and night, summer and winter, sun and moon, sky and earth, the cosmic harmony that they are reenacting, two perfect halves of one whole. Like the Goddess, the bride may create life if she chooses, or she may fashion works of art, objects, crafts, or books. Moreover, she brings the radiant love of the Goddess into a home. Like the Goddess, she is powerful, loving, strong, intuitive, a healer, and a teacher. Like the moon, her womb waxes and wanes each month. She is the maiden of the waxing moon, innocent, independent, and carefree. She is the vital mother of the full moon, voluptuous, sensuous, passionate, and fruitful. She is the mysterious, powerful crone, wise and all-knowing, the incomparable seer who can pierce the veils between the worlds.

The bride should take some time to connect to this part of herself before the wedding, working for several weeks with this loving, expansive energy of the Goddess that dwells within her and which she manifests.

The Groom and the God

The groom represents the God during the ritual. The bride sees the God in her husband and in every man. He is strong and powerful, gentle and loving. He is not afraid of the emotions within, and can express love and tears, happiness and sadness in equal measure. He is the poet, the dancer, and the shaman. He is the fire of the sun, the lord of the hunt, the stag of seven tines, the protector and the protected, the son, the lover, and the husband. He is the wildfire, the wild one of the forest in his heart.

The groom should spend a few weeks before the ceremony connecting with the God, and the God within.

Goddesses of Love

The bride might like to work on building a special bond with one of the goddesses of love in the weeks and months prior to the handfasting. During the ceremony, you can arrange with the celebrant to invoke one of these deities.

Abundia

Abundia is an Italian witch goddess or, some say, queen of the fairies. She appears as a lovely woman with dark hair, wearing a circlet with a star on her forehead. She is a fertility goddess who bestows abundance on earth.

Aine

Aine is an Irish goddess of love and fertility who took many mortal lovers. Her name means "brightness," "heat," or "speed," indicating that she is a sun goddess, and the word *Ain* is cognate with the Latin *ignis,* meaning "fire." Her festival is Midsummer, marked by a torchlight procession about her hill led by young women and a bonfire vigil. When she was pursued by St. Patrick's hounds, she scattered her perfume on meadowsweet to confuse them, and so gave the flower its scent. It is one of the herbs of love.

Akka

Akka (Finnish) is the wife of the supreme god Ukko. Akka is the goddess of the harvest, agriculture, love, women, and female sexuality. She is an Earth Mother goddess.

Aphrodite

Aphrodite is the Greek goddess of love and desire. She is supremely beautiful and no man or woman can resist her charms. Her magic is the rapture of love and sexual ecstasy. She was "foam-born" (*aphros*) from the sea, rising naked and accompanied by doves and sparrows. She sailed to shore on a scallop shell, emerging from the sea near Paphos on the island of Cyprus.

It is likely that Aphrodite was originally an Eastern fertility goddess adopted into the Olympian pantheon. The fact that she renews her virginity in a spring after each sexual encounter proclaims her to be an Earth Mother/fertility goddess, who gives birth each year to the crops and is renewed in the springtime, washed clean by the spring rains. Her domain seems to have encompassed the fertility of animals, plants, and human beings.

As the world grew more patriarchal and prudish, Aphrodite's gifts and orgiastic nature were looked upon with contempt or horror, but originally her rites were sacred. Sex constituted a sacred act and was the proper way to honor the goddess of love and desire. The patriarchal Greeks stripped away all her other attributes, leaving her the goddess of love: ostensibly of married love as Aphrodite Benetrix, encompassing spiritual or ideal love as Aphrodite Urania ("Heavenly Aphrodite"), but also as the goddess of lust and the patroness of prostitutes as Aphrodite Porne. Her chief festival was called the *Aphrodisiac,* a word that is still familiar to us today. Her attributes are the dolphin, dove, swan, pomegranate, sparrow, goose, partridge, wryneck, rose, myrtle, quince, rose campion, water mint, plane, cypress, and bay. Her metal is copper.

Ashtart

Ashtart is the Canaanite goddess of sexuality, fertility, love, war, and the hunt. She is the consort of Baal, and is also a goddess of war and the chase. In Sidon, where she was worshipped, she merited royal priests and priestesses.

Athyr

Athyr (Hindu) gave birth to the universe. She is a goddess of love and beauty.

Bast

Bast is the ancient Egyptian cat-headed goddess of pleasure, fire, childbirth, fertility, joy, sex, music, dance, protection, laughter, healing, intuition, marriage, and animals. She is one of the oldest Egyptian goddesses and the daughter of Ra, and is known as the "Eye of Ra." Herodotus, writing in the mid-fifth century BCE, described the festival at Bubastis in the eastern Delta. He said that 700,000 people (not including children) attended it. They sang and played music, drank wine, and made sacrifices, paying their respects to the goddess in her red granite temple. Dead cats were taken there to be embalmed and buried in order to carry messages from their owners to the gods. Bast was shown dressed in green, holding a sistrum (a rattle) in her right hand and a basket in her left, often with kittens at her feet.

Branwen

Branwen ("White Raven") is the Welsh goddess of love, the sister of the alder god Bran ("Raven"), who was the guardian of all Britain. In the *Mabinogion* stories, she was called a "fair maiden," one of the most beautiful women in the world, and one of the three chief ladies (sovereign goddesses) of the land.

Demeter

Demeter ("Earth Mother") is the Greek goddess of agriculture, fertility, and marriage. Her priestesses initiated bride and groom into the secrets of the marriage bed. Demeter rules the cycle of the year, the phases of the moon, the seasons, and the life of humans, ordering them all in their time. This makes her a goddess of stability, law, and order, a state that extends into fidelity and marriage. The women of Greece celebrated the feast of Thesmophoria (*thesmophoros,* "she of the regular customs") in her honor. In ancient art, Demeter was often portrayed as a solemn woman, wearing a wreath of braided ears of wheat.

Dione

Dione (Greek) is the daughter of Uranus and Gaia and the mother of Aphrodite. She is the goddess of prophecy and love.

Freya

Freya ("Lady," "Mistress") is the Scandinavian goddess who gave her name to the sixth day of the week, Friday. She is usually depicted in a flowing gown and sometimes a feathered cloak and a shining jeweled necklace. She is a goddess of love, and lends a favorable ear to the prayers of lovers. Love songs were always composed in her honor, and in Germany her name became the verb that meant "to woo." She is a goddess of lust; the trickster god Loki accused her of sleeping with all the gods in turn. Freya even mated with Loki in the form of a flea. She enjoys sexual freedom, taking her choice of lovers among gods and mortals at will.

Freya is married to the god Odur, who is a marvelous lover and represents passion and the pleasures of sexual love. He also symbolizes the summer sun. When he is with her, she is happy and content, but he once disappeared and she was forced to hunt for him in a story reminiscent of the search of Demeter for Persephone, and Ishtar for Tammuz. Freya wept tears of gold and amber as she wandered around the world seeking news of his whereabouts. Without the god and goddess, icy winter gripped the earth. Eventually she found Odur beneath a myrtle tree in the southern lands. They were reunited and Freya became as happy as a bride, which is why brides in the northern lands wear myrtle in preference to orange blossom. As they journeyed home, the grass grew green again, the flowers blossomed, and nature rejoiced.

Frigg

Frigg (Norse) is the wife of the chief god Odin. She is a goddess of marriage, fertility, sexuality, love, and motherhood.

Gaia

Gaia (Greek), whose name means "deep-breasted" because of her nurturing qualities, is the Earth itself. She created the universe and the first race of gods and humans. She represents love and fertility, and presides over marriages.

Hathor

Hathor ("House of Horus") is the ancient Egyptian goddess of joy, motherhood, love, beauty (copper mirrors had an image of her on their handles), dance, music, and the arts in general. She protects pregnant women.

Hathor and the falcon-headed god Horus are husband and wife. Their sacred marriage was celebrated on the eighteenth day of Paoni, the tenth month, when the image of Hathor was taken from her temple at Dendera and placed on a barge, which sailed down the Nile to the temple of Horus at Edfu. The image of Horus was taken from Edfu to greet that of Hathor on the river, and thus the two deities were said to consummate their marriage.

Hathor's earliest form was probably the cow. Sometimes she is shown as entirely animal, or as a cow-headed woman, or with a pair of cow horns encircling the solar disc.

Hera

Hera ("Lady," "Protectress") is the Greek goddess of marriage. Zeus found and courted her at Knossos in Crete. She took pity on him when he appeared as a bedraggled cuckoo, and she warmed him in her breast. He immediately assumed his true shape and made love to her, and so afterward they were married. The gods all brought wedding gifts, and the wedding night was spent on Samos and lasted 300 mortal years. Hera bathes in the spring at Canathus, near Argos, to renew her virginity. She carries a pomegranate in her left hand to symbolize the death of the year, and a cuckoo-topped scepter in her right hand to symbolize the regeneration of the year in spring. Her renewal bath has similar connotations.

Ishtar

Ishtar is the Mesopotamian goddess of life and death. She rules sexual activity, ovulation, and the menstrual cycle. She is depicted sitting on a lapis lazuli throne, wearing a necklace with a star and accompanied by doves. Sometimes she is shown riding on a lion, her sacred animal. As a goddess of love, her symbol was the eight-pointed star (the planet Venus) or a rosette. The zodiac was known as the "girdle of Ishtar."

The most famous story of Ishtar tells of her search for Tammuz in the underworld, a legend recorded on clay tablets around 1750 BCE that recalls the search of Demeter for Persephone. Tammuz was Ishtar's husband and died every year during the hot month of Tammuz (July–August), gored by a boar. His soul was taken to the underworld. Ishtar led the lamentation, but the whole world mourned his death. The earth became dry and barren, as all vegetation withered in the blistering heat. Ishtar decided that she must go into the underworld to rescue her husband from the clutches of Ereshkigal, the goddess of the underworld, but despite the fact that she relinquished her clothes and jewels, she also was taken prisoner. Meanwhile, the earth was arid, barren, and joyless. Sin the moon god and Shamash the sun god decided that something had to be done. They asked Ea, the god of water, magic, and wisdom, to help; he sent a messenger into the underworld with a powerful spell. Ereshkigal was forced to release her captives. Ishtar was purified by Ea's waters and passed back through the seven gates, regaining her raiment and jewels at each.[1] Joy returned to earth and life began anew as the first rains fell around the time of the autumn equinox, when the festival of the Holy Marriage was celebrated.

Isis

Isis ("Throne") is the Egyptian goddess of marriage, motherhood, healing, magic, prophecy, love, fertility, agriculture, domestic crafts, and brewing. Like other magical goddesses, Isis is associated with spinning and weaving, drawing out concepts into being, and weaving or knotting various forces to control them. Isis taught humanity the art of using magical knots. It has been said that the priestesses of Isis could control the weather simply by braiding and releasing their hair. One of Isis' symbols is the *tiet,* which is also called the "Isis-knot" and "the Blood of Isis" and is associated with her menstrual blood or womb and vagina. In shape, it looks like an ankh with the arms folded down. It is sometimes considered the knot of fate.

Isis and her husband, the god Osiris, ruled on earth. They taught humankind how to plant and harvest grain, how to spin and weave, and how to make tools, bread, beer, and wine. They also established the institution of marriage, invented religious ritual, and rescued the inhabitants of Egypt from the barbarous custom of cannibalism.

All this time, the kingdom was peaceful and prosperous, but trouble was brewing. Their brother Set grew jealous and hatched a plot with seventy-two co-conspirators to kill Osiris. They invited Osiris to a party. When the festivities were in full swing, Set arranged for a beautiful coffin to be brought into the room, declaring that whoever could perfectly fit into the coffin should own it. Everyone tried it, since it was a magnificent piece of workmanship, but it fitted no one. Then everyone called for the king to try it. Osiris duly stepped into it and lay down. Instantly, the lid was slammed shut and nailed down. Osiris suffocated within and died, going into the afterlife and becoming the ruler of the dead. Set's followers took the coffin and threw it in the Nile, hoping it would sink. Instead, it sailed away. After many adventures, Isis found the coffin and set about reviving Osiris, beating her wings to force air into his lifeless lungs and trying to warm him with her own body, impregnating herself on the erect penis of Osiris and conceiving the child Horus.

Juno

Juno is the Roman queen of heaven and consort of the god Jupiter, invoked as *Optima Maxima,* i.e., "best and greatest goddess." She is the goddess of women, particularly married women, and oversees all aspects of a woman's life from birth, youth, marriage, and child-bearing to death. As the patroness of marriage, Juno restores peace between quarreling couples. Her husband had many affairs, and this was her greatest grief; she insists that fidelity is part of marriage. One of her temples was a refuge for women treated badly by their husbands. She is a mother goddess, possibly of the full moon, and rules childbirth, blessing and guarding every child who is born, according to the Romans. Her own children are Mars, Hebe, and Vulcan. Every year on the first of March, the married women of Rome held a festival called the *Matronalia* to honor the goddess and thank her for her gifts. They prayed for happy marriages and healthy babies.

Lada

Lada (Slavonic) is the goddess of springtime and love worshipped throughout Lithuania, Poland, and Russia. Her husband is Laro, god of pleasure, joy, and marriage.

Maia

Maia (Greek) is one of the famous Pleiades, the seven daughters of Atlas and the nymph Pleione. She is the goddess of the spring, youth, and love. Zeus fell in love with her and fathered a son, the god Hermes.

Olwen

Olwen (Welsh) is a goddess of love and spring. She was the daughter of the giant Hawthorn, who would tolerate no suitor for his daughter as he knew that if she should marry, his life would come to an end. Kulwch, the son of a king, had no need to see her to fall in love with her; he blushed at her very name, and asked her father how he could win her in marriage. Eventually, after some fierce resistance, Hawthorn agreed to discuss the bride price of his daughter: thirteen treasures must be presented to him as a dowry. Though this was a terrible and dangerous task, Kulwch agreed, and after many adventures, the treasures were laid before the incredulous Hawthorn. The marriage of his daughter was, of course, the herald of his death. However, seeing all the quests completed, he turned to Kulwch and said, "My daughter is yours. By my free will you should never have her, for with her I lose my life." Thereupon he suffered his head to be cut off and it was put on a pole. That same night, Olwen was Kulwch's bride.

Oshun

Oshun ("Sweet Water") is the Nigerian goddess of rivers, a deity of fertility, love, beauty, and sensual pleasures, and the patroness of artists, witches, and diviners. Hers are all the feminine powers, and her symbols are the sacred drum, which represents her womb, as well as the crescent moon, the color yellow, mirrors, and cowrie shells. Oshun is usually depicted as a tall, coffee-colored woman, with seven bracelets, a mirror at her belt, carrying a pot of river water, and accompanied by a peacock.

The Yoruba recognized that the cosmos is a perfect construct and contains within it all possibilities. The types of energy within it number 401, with 200 positive energies, 200 negative energies, and one neutral energy that can express itself as either positive or negative. These are called *Orisa,* and each one is a pure energy that may be expressed in human life in myriad ways. Oshun is the Orisa of pure joy, expressed in creativity, sensuality, beauty, childbirth, and wealth.

Qadesh

Qadesh ("Holy") is a Hittite goddess whose worship was introduced into Egypt in the New Kingdom. She is a moon goddess of love, sexual pleasure, and ecstasy. She was depicted as a naked woman standing on the back of a lion and holding flowers (or a mirror) and snakes in her hands.

Sjofna

Sjofna (Norse) is a goddess of love and sex, also known as Vjofn. It was her duty to end quarrels between married couples.

Var

Var (Norse) is a goddess of contracts and agreements who punishes those who break their oaths. She also symbolizes love.

Xochiquetzal

Xochiquetzal (Aztec), whose name means "precious flower," was attractive and desirable, and her gifts were sexual pleasure, flowers, and fertility. Brides braided their hair into a likeness of the two quetzal plumes that were sacred to her.

Gods of Love

Adonis

Adonis (Greek) is the god of vegetation, fertility, and rebirth, and the consort of Aphrodite. The cult of this vegetation god is generally thought to have originated in Syria, and his name is a variation on the Semitic *Adonai,* simply meaning "Lord." According to the most complete version of his story, the mortal King Cinyras boasted that his daughter Myrrha ("Myrrh") was more beautiful than Aphrodite, the goddess of love. As a punishment, the gods caused the unfortunate Myrrha to fall in love with her father. She tricked him into sleeping with her and getting her pregnant. When the king discovered what had happened, he was overcome with disgust and guilt, and took up his sword to kill her.

Myrrha fled from the palace, but her father caught up with her on the brow of a hill. Just as he lifted the blade to strike her, the goddess

Aphrodite took pity on the girl and instantly changed her into a myrrh tree, which the sword cleaved in two.[2] Out tumbled the infant Adonis. Aphrodite concealed the lovely boy inside a chest, which she asked Persephone, the queen of the underworld, to look after.

Overwhelmed by curiosity, Persephone peeped inside the chest and instantly fell in love with the handsome youth she found there. When Aphrodite demanded that she return Adonis to her, Persephone refused, wanting to keep him for herself. Eventually the two goddesses appealed to Zeus (the king of the gods) to settle the quarrel. He appointed the muse Calliope to make the ruling, and she decided that Aphrodite should have Adonis for one-third of the year, Persephone for another third, and that he should have one-third to himself.

However, Aphrodite was not happy with this and decided to cheat. She donned her magic girdle, which caused all that looked upon her beauty to fall hopelessly in love with her; as a result, Adonis wanted to be with her all the time. Persephone reported this to Aphrodite's usual lover, the war god Ares, who flared up in a jealous rage. He transformed himself into a wild boar and tore Adonis to pieces.[3] From each drop of blood that fell, a red flower bloomed.[4] However, Adonis was an immortal god of vegetation, and so was reborn each spring.

Zeus resolved to put an end to the squabbling and mayhem, and decreed that Adonis must spend the winter with Persephone, but could spend the summer with Aphrodite. When Adonis was with his beloved Aphrodite, the land bloomed and the people rejoiced, but when he was with Persephone in the underworld, winter came and the people mourned. As in other fertility religions, it was the mating of the young god and goddess that made the earth blossom and fruit.

Aengus Mac Og

Aengus Mac Og (Irish) is a young god of love. He is the son of the good god the Dagda, and Boann, goddess of the River Boyne and one of the Tuatha de Danaan. He lived in the tumulus of Newgrange in County Meath. His name means something like "vigorous son of youth."

In the story of the Vision of Aengus (*Aislinge Oenguso*), he saw a lovely maiden in his dreams; before he could touch her she disappeared. These dreams went on for a year, and he became sick with love for her. His mother searched the length and breadth of Ireland in an attempt to find the girl, but without success. Eventually, she summoned the Dagda to help, and the girl was located at the Galtee Mountains in Co. Tipperary. Her name was Caer Iobharmheith. It was explained to them that she was a swan maiden who lived in the form of a bird on alternate years. They found her at Lough Beal Dragan at Samhain, accompanied by 150 maidens linked by a silver chain. Her chain was of gold. Aengus became a swan himself, and they embraced and flew three times around the lake, putting everyone in the vicinity asleep with their songs.

Aengus rescued the Irish hero Diarmaid and his mistress Grainne as they fled from her aged husband Fionn and his men. On another occasion, Aengus blew four kisses into the air, which changed into four birds, which charmed the young people of Ireland.

Agni
Agni (Hindu) is the god of fire, purity, and fertility and is associated with sex and male virility. He loves all his worshippers equally, visiting their hearths.

Anteros
Anteros (Roman) is the god of mutual love who punishes those who do not return love.

Cernunnos
Cernunnos (Gaulish) is a god of fertility, animals, wild places, love, birth, death, and rebirth. He is depicted as a stag-headed man holding a torc in one hand and a snake in the other.

Cupid

Cupid (Roman) is the god of physical love and the son of Venus, and is usually equated with the Greek Eros. His name comes from *cupido,* meaning "desire," and he was also known as Amor, or "love." He wore a blindfold to suggest that the arrows of love he shot into human beings hit at random in a way often considered to be mischievous.

Eros

Eros (Greek) was considered to be the son of Aphrodite and is the god of sex and desire, his name giving us the word *erotic.* He has a golden bow and arrows, which he fires at humans and gods alike, making them fall in love. According to the Greek poet Hesiod, Eros was one of the first deities born into the world. In his *Theogony,* Hesiod claims that Eros emerged from the primeval chaos, along with Gaia (the earth) and Tartarus (the underworld), and:

> . . . Eros, the fairest of the deathless gods;
> he unstrings the limbs and subdues both mind
> and sensible thought in the breasts of all gods and all men.

This makes it clear that neither god nor man can resist the influence of Eros, making him one of the most powerful of the gods.

Faunus

Faunus (Roman) is the Roman nature god, comparable to the Greek Pan, and patron of the fields and shepherds. The whispering of the wind in the trees is his voice. He is the leader of the Fauni, the Italian nature fairies. Like many nature spirits he is half man, half goat in appearance. His female counterpart is called Fauna or Faula.

Fu-Hsing

Fu-Hsing (Chinese) is the god of love, success, and good fortune. He is also called Fuk, the star god of happiness and wealth. His sacred animal is the bat.

Kama

Kama (Hindu) is the god of love who sprang directly from the heart of Brahma, the creator, or some say he is the son of Lakshmi. Kama is the god of love, lust, and desire and is married to Rati, the goddess of sexual desire, and to Priti, the goddess of pleasure. He has a bow made of sugar cane strung with honeybees, and five flower-tipped arrows that inflame the five senses and inspire love in anyone they hit. His chief festival is the Madonatsava, and he is invoked by brides when they leave the parental home. He gives his name to the *Kama Sutra,* a work on erotic techniques. In Hindu marriage rituals, a part of the hymns refer to him. Kama and Rati bring with them the cuckoo, the bee, spring, and a gentle breeze.

Krishna

Krishna (Indian) is the eighth incarnation of the god Vishnu and enjoyed many thousands of amorous adventures with women, despite his enduring love for his consort Radha. He grew up in Brindavan, playing many pranks, performing miraculous deeds, and sporting with milkmaids, whom he charmed with his flute, making them fall madly in love with him. Krishna is believed to have defeated numerous dragons and monsters, and eventually, as predicted, killed his half uncle, the tyrannical king Kamsa.

Liber

Liber (Roman) is the god of wild places, nature, fertility, wine, and passionate sex.

Maponus

Maponus (British) is the god of youth and love who corresponds to the Welsh Mabon and the Irish Aengus, and is identified with the Roman Apollo. He is also the deity of poetry and music. He was the tutelary god of the Brigantes tribe.

Pan

Pan (Greek) is the god of fertility, wild places, flocks, animals, and male sexuality, lust, and love. Pan is the son of the god Hermes by Oeneis, a nymph of Arcadia. The ancient writer Servius described him as being:

> . . . formed in the likeness of nature with horns to resemble the rays of the sun and the horns of the moon; his face is ruddy in the imitation of ether; he wears a spotted fawn skin resembling the stars in the sky; his lower limbs are hairy because of the trees and wild beasts; he has the feet of a goat to resemble the stability of the earth; his pipe has seven reeds in accordance with the harmony of heaven; his pastoral staff bears a crook in reference to the year which curves back on itself, and finally, he is the god of all Nature.

Pan roams the mountains, pursuing game in the valleys and playing his pipe in the groves. Travelers in the woods often hear his music. His call is said to give rise to "panic," an overwhelming fear in all that hear it.

Pothos

Pothos (Greek) is a winged god of sexual yearning, love, passion, and desire.

Gay Weddings

The symbolism of gay handfastings may be rather different from heterosexual unions. Rather than express the polarity of male and female, God and Goddess, you may wish to explore the symbolism and mythology of homosexual gods and goddesses.

Apollo

Apollo (Greek) is the god of the sun, healing, poetry, and divination. Apollo seems to have been attracted to both male and female lovers. For one tale of his love for a youth, see *Zephyrus*.

Artemis

Artemis (Greek) is the daughter of Zeus, king of the Greek gods, and Leto, one of Zeus' many mistresses. Artemis was worshipped by the warrior Amazons as the new moon goddess. When she was a little girl, Zeus wanted to give her a gift and asked her what she wanted. The goddess replied, "I want to run forever, wild and free, with my hounds in the woods and never, ever marry." She hunted and killed any men who dared defile her mysteries. After marriage, women were not allowed to give her offerings.

Artemis is the goddess that women call upon when they are in trouble or abused. She befriends the abused and punishes the abuser. Within every woman the spirit of Artemis exists, independent and confident. She doesn't deny her own nature to satisfy another.

Catamitus

Catamitus (Roman) was a beautiful youth loved by Jupiter, in a parallel tale to the story of Ganymede and Zeus. The word *catamite* was once used to describe gay men.

Diana

Diana (Roman) is a maiden goddess of the moon and hunt, armed with a crescent-moon bow and arrows. She is a personification of nature, roaming through the moonlit wilds, followed by her dancing nymph disciples. Late Roman sources and the inquisitors of the Middle Ages described her as the leader of the witches.

Eros

Eros (Greek) is the god of both heterosexual and homosexual love. For more on Eros, see the previous section, "Gods of Love."

Ganymede

Ganymede (Greek) was a youthful prince of Troy. He caught the eye of Zeus, the king of the gods, who took the shape of an eagle to seize the boy and carry him to Olympus, where Ganymede acted as his cup bearer. His jealous wife Hera insisted that Zeus send the boy away, and he eventually agreed, but first he made Ganymede immortal, setting him in the stars as the constellation of Aquarius.

Hyacinthus

(Greek). See *Zephyrus*.

Zephyrus

Zephyrus (Greek) is the god of the wind who was jealous of Apollo's love for the youth Hyacinthus and the time they spent together. One day, Apollo and Hyacinthus were playing quoits. Apollo threw a disc, but Zephyrus blew it off course and it struck the boy's head, killing him. Distraught that he had killed his friend, Apollo turned him into a flower.

Transexual Deities

Ardhanarishvara

Ardhanarishvara (Hindu) is a deity, half man and half woman, with the right side representing Shiva and the left side Parvati. The male side wears a leopard skin and has a serpent coiling around his arm, while the female side wears an orange skirt, a scarf, and plenty of jewelry.

Harihara

Harihara (Hindu) is a god born of the union of the male deities Shiva and Vishnu. His name means "Golden Ravisher" and he is shown with Vishnu occupying the female, left half of his body, and Shiva the male, right half. He is the guardian of highways who may bring or take away blight.

1. Witches will recognize this story as the descent of the Goddess into the underworld.

2. Myrrh was a well-known aphrodisiac, and the birth of Adonis from myrrh indicates the orgiastic nature of his rites. The drops of gum shed by the myrrh represent the tears shed for him during the Adonia Festival.

3. In some versions of the tale it is Artemis, the goddess of hunt and moon, who causes his death.

4. These red flowers were identified as anemones or red roses.

Chapter 5

CHOOSING THE MOMENT

*A*s a Pagan, you will want to choose the most auspicious and magical moment for your handfasting. Magicians believe that there are tides of waxing and waning energies related to the phases of the moon, the positions of the planets, and the time of year. If you begin a venture when the energies are waning, you will be swimming against the tide of power, and you will find that difficulties and obstacles strew your path. If you begin when the energies are waxing or full, everything will flow more easily, and you will be more likely to succeed. Handfasting is one of the most important magical rites that you will ever engage in, just as choosing a partner is one of the most crucial decisions you will ever make in your life.

According to the Phase of the Moon

Witches practice magic according to the phases of the moon. The moon was the earliest method of measuring the passage of time. Its waxing and waning marked off the days, and the root word for moon, *mene,* still gives us our words for month, measurement, and menstruation. While the moon is a constant presence in the night sky, it is ever changing. Women often feel an identity with the moon; the menstrual cycle begins in youth, and the womb waxes and wanes, bleeding each month until the onset of menopause, and the belly swells like a full moon during pregnancy. So the phases of the moon can be seen as reflected in the life of women and the ever present but ever changing Great Goddess herself: the waxing moon as maiden, the full moon as pregnant mother, and the waning moon as old wise woman.

From the moon we learn that each thing has its season—a time to be born, a time to grow, a time to wither, and a time to die and pass back into the void. It is important to recognize the moment for an idea, project, or relationship to be born, the point to bring it to maturity, and the time to let it go. All things are constantly in flux, but come again in their season.

People often speak of the three phases of the moon, but it actually has four phases—three visible phases (waxing, full, and waning) and then three days in darkness.

Waxing Moon

The waxing (growing) moon is a good time for starting new projects and relationships and for planting flowers and vegetables. It is a time for beginnings, things that will grow to fullness in the future. The waxing moon may be a lucky time for a handfasting, representing your hopes for what is yet to come.

Full Moon

The full moon is a good time for positive magic—healing, blessing, and so on. It is a very creative period and you will feel the benefit when working on imaginative projects such as writing, painting, or composing music. The energy of the full moon celebrates the fertile, positive, creative forces in the world and in relationships and is a good time for a handfasting.

Waning Moon

The waning (shrinking) moon is a time for letting go of bad habits, negative thinking, etc. It is a time of winding down, relinquishing old relationships and situations. It is the time to perform purifications and cleansing magic. It is also the time for a handparting, the ending of a relationship, rather than a handfasting.

Dark Moon

During the three days of the dark moon, the moon regenerates itself and begins life anew, just as all life generates in the darkness of the womb or seeds in the dark earth. The moon then grows to maturity in the light, before aging and dying and returning to the darkness, where life begins again, month after month, season after season, year after year. The days of the dark moon are good for deep inner journeys and meditations rather than the outward expression of the life journey. This is not really a suitable time for a handfasting.

According to the Time of Day

I once went to a handfasting held at Handfast Point, a cliff overlooking the sea in the south of England. It was held at dawn as the sun came up, a powerful symbol of new beginnings. However, it might mean more to you to be married at midday, representing the zenith of the day's power, or at dusk, when the Otherworld is near. Maybe you would like to marry at the witching hour of midnight, or at the time you first met. Choose the symbolism that is right for you and your relationship.

According to the Sabbat

The eight Pagan Sabbats of witches represent the waxing and waning of the solar year. Though the feminine energy of the Goddess is present throughout the cycle, the power of the God ebbs and flows throughout the year. The eight Sabbats mark his life cycle. He is born at the winter solstice, is nursed at Imbolc, grows to manhood at Ostara, marries the Goddess at Beltane, fertilizes her at Midsummer, is honored as high king at Lughnasa, sacrifices himself for the greater good at Herfest (the autumn equinox), rules the land of the dead at Samhain, and comes to rebirth at Yule.

As the summer sun, the God brings fertility, sexual power, and fruitfulness. The mating of the sun and earth brings about the flowering and fruiting of Mother Earth.

Imbolc/Candlemas

Imbolc ("in the belly"), or Candlemas, celebrates the first stirrings of spring, around February 2. This is a festival of the waxing year, when the sun is growing stronger and the days longer, and the first shoots force their way through the frozen earth. New lambs are born in the fields and ewes come into milk, a symbol of purity and nurturing, respectively. This festival is dedicated to the maiden goddess of spring, and some consider it inappropriate for a handfasting. However, in Celtic myth it is dedicated to the triple goddess Brighid, or Bride, perhaps the origin of our word *bride,* so others think it entirely suitable. During this time, the young God moves through childhood and approaches puberty.

Ostara

Ostara celebrates the vernal equinox, spring, and the growing light, around March 21. Wiccans see this as the time when the young God and Goddess meet as youth and maid. It is a lucky time for a wedding, with vital life burgeoning throughout nature. Leaves unfurl on the trees, sun-colored daffodils bloom in the hedgerows, and animals prepare nests, ready for mating.

Beltane

Beltane ("bright-fire") marks the start of summer and fertility, around May 1. May has been considered an unlucky month in which to marry for a number of reasons. This season was considered to be the time of the sacred marriage of the gods, and was therefore taboo for human weddings. Beltane is a festival of death as well as rebirth, the death of winter and the birth of summer. Though Bel is a god of summer fire, he is also the winter ruler of the dead. In ancient Rome, the Feast of the Dead and the festival of the goddess of chastity both occurred in May, neither appropriate times to hold a wedding. However, many modern witches and Pagans see this as a fortuitous time for handfasting, with the flowering of the year.

Midsummer/Coamhain

Midsummer, or Coamhain, is the time of the summer solstice, the zenith of the sun and summer, around June 21. The month of June is traditionally a lucky time for weddings as it is sacred to (and named after) Juno, the Roman goddess of marriage.

Lughnasa/Lammas

Lughnasa, or Lammas, is the beginning of the harvest, marking the prime of the Corn Lord, around August 2. This was the traditional time for handfastings among the ancients, carried out at the annual clan gatherings or fairs.

The Autumn Equinox/Herfest

Herfest celebrates the autumn equinox, the harvest festival, the death of the Corn Lord, and waning of the sun, around September 21. From this point in the cycle until Yule, the Lord is absent, so this is not a good time for a marriage.

Samhain

Samhain marks the start of winter, the festival of the dead, around October 31. The contracting energies of Samhain are concerned with dissolution, death, winter, and the spirits of the ancestors. For Wiccans, this is the time when the God rules as lord of the dead in the underworld, lying in the earth-womb of the Goddess. This is not a lucky time for a wedding.

Yule

Yule is the time of the winter solstice, the rebirth of the sun, around December 21, and the start of the waxing year. This is the time when the God is reborn and energy flows back into the world. It is a good festival on which to celebrate a handfasting.

Though it might not be appropriate to marry on a Sabbat associated with waning sun energies, if you cannot wait for the next appropriate Sabbat, you might choose another day in the same month on a waxing or full moon.

According to the Month

Some of the ancient Pagan beliefs found their way into popular wedding lore in more recent times. Victorian brides were warned, "Marry in the month of May, and you'll live to rue the day," an old taboo from Pagan times. Even Queen Victoria prevented her children from marrying in May, and April 30 was a busy time for vicars, with brides trying to marry before the May prohibition began.

An old rhyme states:

Married when the year is new, he'll be loving, kind, and true.
When February birds do mate, you wed nor dread your fate.
If you wed when March winds blow, joy and sorrow both you'll know.
Marry in April when you can, joy for Maiden and for Man.
Marry in the month of May, and you'll live to rue the day.

Marry when June roses grow, over land and sea you'll go.
Those who in July do wed, must labour for their daily bread.
Whoever wed in August be, many a change is sure to see.
Marry in September's shrine, your living will be rich and fine.
If in October you do marry, love will come but riches tarry.
If you wed in bleak November, only joys will come, remember.
When December snows fall fast, marry and true love will last.

Remember that this rhyme is just Victorian whimsy and has little basis in real magical lore. I have only included it for fun.

According to the Day of the Week

According to an old English rhyme, different days of the week are lucky or unlucky for weddings:

Monday for wealth
Tuesday for health
Wednesday the best day of all
Thursday for losses
Friday for crosses
Saturday for no luck at all

The favorite day on which to be married was Sunday, until the Puritans made this illegal. The unluckiest day of all was Saturday, the very time when most weddings take place today. This may be because it is the day of Saturn, the planet that is concerned with endings, dissolution, and death. Friday was also considered unlucky among Christians, as Christ was crucified on a Friday; though for Pagans, Friday is the day of Venus, the planet of love, sacred in ancient times to the ancient Goddess of Love in her various guises. She is always associated with the sea, and it is for this reason that fish was eaten on Fridays, a custom later adopted by Christians.

You can also take the planetary rulers of the days into account:

Sunday (ruled by the Sun)
Sunday rules employers, friendship, healing, and work. It is named after the sun and is sacred to the Sun God, who rules fertility, passion, and sexual energy.

Monday (ruled by the Moon)
Monday rules agriculture, psychic ability, witchcraft, the home, and medicine. It is named after the moon and is sacred to the Moon Goddess, who rules fertility, feminine power, and the emotions, including love.

Tuesday (ruled by the planet Mars)
Tuesday rules conflict, competition, debates, courage, and lust. It is named after the Norse war god Tiw.

Wednesday (ruled by the planet Mercury)
Wednesday rules study, teaching, divination, and communications. It is named after the northern chief god Woden, who rules expansive energies, bards, and divination.

Thursday (ruled by the planet Jupiter)
Thursday rules material things, money, property, and luck. It is named after the northern storm god Thor.

Friday (ruled by the planet Venus)
Friday rules love, art, music, incense, and perfume making. It is named after Freya, or Frigg, the northern goddess of love.

Saturday (ruled by the planet Saturn)
Saturday rules the elderly, death, reincarnation, wills, destruction, and endings. It is named after the Roman god Saturn.

Chapter 6

HANDFASTING THEMES

$\mathcal{T}$here is no need to choose a theme for your handfasting or elaborate the proceedings in any way, but you might like to include traditions and costumes from your cultural heritage, or explore meaningful Pagan symbolism in your ceremony.

Simple Pagan

The ritual of handfasting does not need to be complicated or expensive; its purpose is for the couple to declare their intentions in front of witnesses and the Old Gods. You might make a simple circle of flowers or crystals in your house or in an open space, invite friends and family to be present, and follow the ceremony with a celebratory meal for which everyone brings food and drink to share. This can be the loveliest handfasting of all. Some simple Pagan handfasting rites are given in chapter 3.

Formal Wiccan

For Wiccans, the handfasting is usually a formal ritual held in front of the entire coven. Non-Wiccans may watch from outside the circle, or inside if they and your high priestess agree. Participants are robed, with the bride and groom wearing colored robes for the occasion (the traditional color for the bride is red) and wearing chaplets of flowers and ivy. Sometimes colored sashes are worn. The Wiccan handfasting rite is given in chapter 3.

As Sun and Moon

You might like to explore the symbolism of the marriage of the God and Goddess as sun and moon, and dress the circle and participants accordingly. The groom would dress in gold and wear symbols of the sun, with crystals such as amber, topaz, and tiger's-eye. The bride might wear silver for the moon, and adorn her brow with a crescent moon and wear gems such as moonstones, pearls, or opals. The time for this wedding would be Beltane, Midsummer, or Yule, preferably at the full or waxing moon.

As Sky and Earth

The God and Goddess also represent the sky and earth, respectively. It is the fertilizing rain of the Sky Father that causes the Earth Mother to flower and bring forth grain. Again, you might explore the symbolism of this in your ritual, with the groom dressed in blue and wearing sun and lightning/thunder symbols, and the bride in green and adorned with flowers and grain. The best time for this would be Ostara, Beltane, Midsummer, or Lughnasa.

Roman

If you worship the Roman gods, are of Italian ancestry, or are just very interested in the ancient Romans, then you might like to incorporate some of the customs of an ancient Roman wedding into your handfasting. The bride was attended by a matron of honor and the groom by a best man who also acted as priest. The bride prepared for the wedding by symbolically renouncing her childhood, giving up her childish toys and maiden's dress (even if the bride isn't a young maiden, some of the imagery of this might be employed).

The ceremony largely revolved around the veiling of the bride, and the term describing a married woman, *nupta,* means "I veil myself." The wedding was called the *nuptiae,* and from this we get our modern word *nuptials.* The bride wore a long, flame-colored, transparent veil called a *flammeum,* which was secured by a wreath. Unlike the modern bridal veil, it did not cover her face. She also wore a white tunic fastened by a girdle, which the groom had the fun of untying on the wedding night. Her hair was divided into six strands, fastened with fillets on top of her head in a cone. During the styling, the hair was parted with a bent-iron spearhead to drive evil spirits from her.

The bride's parents handed her over to the groom with some exchange of vows (you can write your own). The matron of honor would then join the couple's hands. They would make an offering to the gods together and the contract was signed by witnesses. The *cena,* or wedding breakfast, followed, during which gifts would be given to the happy couple.

The wedding procession then ensued, from the bride's home to the groom's, consisting of the bride, groom, three male attendants, and other guests. It began with a representational seizing of the bride from her mother's arms by the groom. Guests would make the kind of suggestive jokes and comments that are still made at weddings today. One of the male attendants would carry a torch lit from the bride's hearth, which would be used to light a fire at her new home. Walnuts were thrown at the couple as a fertility ritual. The bride carried a distaff or spindle. At some point, the procession split so that the groom could hurry to his house in order to be there first to greet the bride.

When the procession arrived at the house, the torches were thrown away, and the bride rubbed the doorway with fat and oil and wreathed it with wool. She was carried over the threshold so that she should not trip, which would be unlucky. She then touched some water and the hearth fire. Inside was a miniature marriage bed for the spirits of the bride and groom to consummate their joining. Songs were then sung to encourage the couple to consummate the marriage in a chamber decorated with fertility symbols, greenery, and fruit. The matron of honor, a married woman herself, led the bride into it and wished the couple perpetual harmony.

Saxon

Very little is known of Saxon marriage rites. However, the Roman historian Tacitus wrote a description of the German tribes and their customs in the first century BCE in his *Germania*. He said that rather than the wife bringing a dowry to the husband, the groom paid a dowry to his wife in the form of a team of oxen, or maybe a shield or lance. This was called the *morgengifu,* or morning gift, and was hers to keep and use as she wished. It signified the she and her husband were jointly responsible for the fecundity of their land and its safety. In return the bride gave her husband a gift of arms.

Viking

Viking weddings were traditionally held on a Friday, the day sacred to Freya, or Frigg, the goddess of love. Ceremonies often lasted for a week or more, and included the drinking of a special bridal ale brewed with honey. The bride and groom drank this for the next month, a period called the *honey moon,* and this is where we get the word.

Before the wedding, the bride was purified by her attendants in a ritual bath and dressed in a gown, a blue cloak, and the bridal crown, woven from corn and flowers. The groom also underwent a ritual bath and was instructed by the older, married men on his duties as a husband and father, and given advice. He dressed in his best clothes and wore his ancestral sword.

On the wedding day, the dowries were exchanged and the wedding took place at an open-air site. The bride was accompanied by a young kinsman bearing a new sword as a present for her husband. The gods were invoked and honored with offerings. The groom then presented the bride with the sword of his ancestors to be held in trust by her for their descendants, symbolizing the family line, protection, and tradition. She then gave him the new sword so that he might protect her and their future family with it. Next, the couple exchanged rings, with the bride's ring offered to her on the hilt of her husband's new sword. They then both placed their hands on the sword hilt and exchanged vows.

Afterward there was a race, or "bride running," to the feasting hall. The last party there may have had to serve the others at the feast.[1]

Medieval

A medieval theme for a handfasting is becoming increasingly popular, as many venues offer medieval-style banquets and entertainment. In medieval times, the rich enjoyed sumptuous weddings celebrated with enormous feasts and jousting contests.

The bride may wear a long gown with wide sleeves and a veil fixed by a fillet of silver, or a wreath of flowers. The groom may dress in doublet and hose. The colors of male and female attire were often matched, the most prestigious colors being purple, crimson, and royal blue, expensive dyes that only the rich could afford. Both men and women wore ribbons tied around their arms or pinned to their costumes. Men wore small posies of herbs pinned to their doublets, and the bridesmaids carried nosegays of scented herbs and flowers. The bride might have sprigs of rosemary in her bouquet or in her bridal wreath. At her wedding to Henry VIII in 1540, Anne of Cleves wore a gold coronet encircled with sprigs of rosemary. Records tell us that some medieval brides carried a little bouquet of gilded marigolds that were dipped in rosewater. The marigolds were thought to have aphrodisiac qualities and were eaten after the ceremony.

To reinforce the medieval theme, use heraldic banners, metal goblets, and candles on tall iron sconces. If the event or wedding feast takes place indoors, decorate with banners, ivy, flowers, and weaponry such as swords, axes, and so on. You can use recorded music or hire minstrels to serenade you with lute and pipes.

Scottish

Those of Scottish ancestry may wish to celebrate accordingly. The bride and groom might like to wear outfits of a tartan pattern. There are many tartans, each associated with a particular family or clan, though this is a relatively modern correlation, dating from Victorian times. The ancient Celts certainly had patterned cloth, but colors were expensive: the king was allowed to have seven different shades in his material, druids six, nobles four,[2] slaves only had one color, while peasants had two.[3] The groom might like to wear a plaid (pronounced "plad"), which is the material used to make the kilt. Contrary to popular opinion, plaid is not the same as tartan. The old kilt was not a simple pleated skirt, but consisted of twelve yards of material wrapped around the waist and fastened with a belt, crossed over the breast and fastened on the left shoulder with a brooch, taking care to leave the right sword arm free.

The rings could be engraved with the words *Mo ghaol ort,* or "I love you" in Scots Gaelic. The bride might wear a traditional Luckenbooth brooch, a pin of engraved silver in the shape of a heart or two hearts entwined, which is given to her by the groom. Afterward this brooch is pinned to the blanket of their first child for luck. A must for the bride, groom, and guests is some white heather, considered lucky all over Britain.

The party might include Scottish music with bagpipes and traditional dances, with the bride and groom leading off a foursome reel with the bridesmaid and best man. Plenty of food and drink should be supplied, especially whisky, for the feast should go on all day and through the night.

Here is a traditional wedding blessing:

A thousand welcomes to you with your marriage kerchief,
May you be healthy all your days.
May you be blessed with long life and peace,
May you grow old with goodness and with riches.

In Scotland, it was traditional for the bride to "walk with the sun," circling the church three times "sunwise" for good luck. This undoubtedly dates from an older Pagan tradition in which she walked three times deosil (clockwise) around the sacred circle or holy ground in an act of positive magic.

Irish

If you follow an Irish Celtic path or have Irish blood, you might like to have a proper Celtic day, with embroidered knotwork costumes and a *ceilidh,* or dance, to follow.

Lady Wilde described an old rustic Irish wedding witnessed by a traveler in Kerry in the early 1800s that seems very Pagan in character.[4] It took place under a hawthorn tree, which was decorated with ribbons and rush candles among the branches. A group of boys marching slowly with flutes, reed pipes, a tin drum, and bone rattles processed to the tree, followed by a boy with a blazing torch, and behind him the couple hand in hand. A canopy of dark cloth was held over them, and two attendants held over their heads a sieve filled with meal, obviously a fertility charm to ensure plenty in their future lives. The guests followed, singing and dancing and waving green leafy branches. The procession moved to the bonfire and circled it three times. Then the black cloth was lifted from over the bridal pair, and they kissed each other, while the guests applauded and cheered, waving their branches. This was followed by feasting and drinking, and no doubt the party lasted all night.

Food might include Irish soda bread, champ (mashed potatoes with spring onions), and fruit cake with almonds, raisins, cherries, and spice. There should be plenty of whiskey and Guinness to drink.

On arriving at her future home, the bride was met on the threshold by her bridegroom's mother, who broke an oaten cake over her head, a good augury of plenty in the future.

You might have the rings engraved with *A rún mo chroí,* which translates as "O love of my heart," or *A mhuirnín dílis,* meaning "O true sweetheart."

Romany

Gypsy marriage customs vary greatly from country to country and even from region to region. Among many, the marriage was celebrated after a pretended elopement; it was customary for the groom to ask the bride's father for the hand of his daughter, and for the father to make a show of refusing. In other families, the suitor was tested by being made to fight members of the girl's family, or by being sent off to steal a sheep or a horse.

The *abiav,* or wedding, has little religious content. Often no formal ritual is necessary, and the couple just agree in front of witnesses to live together, joining hands in the presence of the chief of the tribe or another elder. Jumping over the broomstick was a common practice in some places, and a flowering broom plant was often used. Some couples joined hands over a stream and drank from the same cup, which was broken afterwards. Another tradition was for the bride and groom to prick their fingers with a thorn and then to place a drop of blood on a little piece of bread, which was eaten by their spouse. Alternatively, bread and salt were placed on the knees of the seated bride; the groom then took some of the bread and dipped it into the salt before eating it, or bread was dipped into salt and then broken over the heads of the couple. The gypsy woman wears red on her wedding day as a symbol that she is still a virgin.

India

In a custom reminiscent of a Western stag night, the groom spends his last night of freedom with his male friends. They eat a meal and perform a ritual purification of the groom by pouring water from a jug over him. Turmeric paste (a yellow spice) is rubbed onto his face and chest to give him a sunny glow, which wards off evil spirits. The bride is painted with elaborate henna patterns by her attendants.

At the ceremony, the groom's brother sprinkles flower petals over the couple. He then takes a coconut, which represents fertility, and holds it over the heads of the bride and groom, and circles it three times.

Serbia

The groom's father issues the wedding invitations by going from house to house with a flask of brandy. Guests are invited to toast the couple and give the messenger a small present for his trouble. On the wedding morning, the best man must retrieve a gourd and a handkerchief from the top of a tree before the groom is allowed to enter the bride's house.

Jewish

The bride and groom clasp hands as a sign of their bond. The groom gives the celebrant a handkerchief containing six coins, which he hands over to the bride's father as a symbolic bride price. The couple drink from a glass, which is then broken as a sign that what has been done cannot be undone.

China

In China, red is the color of love and luck, so the bridal dress, the invitations, and even the sheets on the marriage bed are red. Red candles and lamps may also be used. Rice wine is traditional. Chinese brides receive presents of gold jewelry from their female relatives.

Denmark

As soon as the groom is alone, all the women at the celebration try to kiss him. When he leaves the room, all the men try to steal kisses from the bride. In a dance, the groom's relatives circle him and cut up his tie. The traditional wedding cake is the cornucopia cake of almond and marzipan decorated with marzipan portraits of the bride and groom.

Turkey

After the wedding ceremony, the couple must remain apart for twenty-four hours, and then the groom must run the gauntlet to the room where his love awaits while his friends throw old shoes at him. The bride and groom then share some sugar as a sign of the sweetness to come.

Philippines

A white silk cord is placed around the couple's shoulders to indicate their union. At some point in the ceremony, white doves are released to symbolize peace and happiness for the bride and groom in their new life together.

Yugoslavia

One old ceremony in the former Yugoslavia consisted of a torchlight procession that accompanied a young girl to three fountains. She had to take a mouthful of water from one and carry it to the next, and so on. At the last fountain, she carried the water in her mouth back to the bride's home, where she spat it into a jug, which was used for the bride's ritual purification.

Africa

If you are of an African heritage, then be sure to sew some cowrie shells into your wedding costume. These symbolize fertility, beauty, purification, wealth, and power.

The ancestors are invited to be present and a libation is poured as an offering to them. Fill a cup with water and explain that you are pouring it on the ground, in the north, east, south, and west, to honor your ancestors. Water is the source of life and its nourishment. It is used for purification and to symbolize the sustenance of the spirit.

Armenia

The bride dresses in red silk and has feathered wings as a headdress. The guests throw coins at her.

Belgium

The bride embroiders her name on a handkerchief and carries it on her wedding day, and then frames it.

Bermuda

The wedding cake is topped with a sapling tree. The couple plant this in their garden and watch it grow as their relationship develops.

Bohemia

The groom gives the bride a girdle with three keys, a fur cap, and a silver wedding ring. She gives him an embroidered shirt and a wedding ring. The best man wraps the groom in the bride's cloak to keep evil spirits from getting between the couple and causing trouble.

Croatia

After the ceremony, the bride's veil is removed by the married women present and replaced with an apron and headscarf to show her new status. They then sing to her, and she has to walk three times around the well and throw three apples into it for fertility.

Czechoslovakia

Friends plant a tree in the bride's garden and decorate it with painted eggs and ribbons. This is a symbol of fertility, and it is said that the bride will live as long as the tree.

England

In times past, the bride's party walked to the church led by a girl strewing petals on the road, symbolizing a sweet path for the bride. The bride carried a lucky horseshoe, though nowadays these are made of silver or cardboard. Then she must have "Something old, something new, something borrowed, something blue, and a silver sixpence in her shoe," according to a Victorian rhyme. Something old represents continuity with the past, something new is a token of her new future and altered status, and something borrowed is a token of friendship. Blue was the color of the Goddess in ancient times, though many modern brides do not realize why they have to wear blue! The silver sixpence in the shoe represents wealth and plenty. Sixpences are no longer made, so the bride has to be content with a silver fivepence piece, unless the family has an old sixpence lying around somewhere. If she finds a spider in her wedding dress, this is considered very lucky.

Finland

The bride wears a golden crown, which later on she must place on another's head while blindfolded. Whoever is crowned will be the next to marry. At the reception, the bride holds a sieve covered with a shawl, and the guests put presents of money into it.

France

Many couples drink the bridal toast from the *coupe de marriage,* a two-handled loving cup.

Modern Greece

Today, the *koumbaros,* or best man, adorns the couple with crowns of white or gold, or crowns made from flowers or twigs and vines wrapped in silver paper. To ensure a sweet life, the bride carries some sugar.

Ancient Egypt

The ancient Egyptians were probably the first to have laws covering marriage, which they considered to be both a spiritual and legal arrangement. The laws covered the rights and duties of the couple, including the right of divorce for both men and women. Marriage contracts were signed by three witnesses, and included the name of the couple, the names of both sets of parents, the professions of husband and wife, and the signature of the scribe who drew up the contract, plus details of any settlement—a prenuptial agreement—to be made in the case of divorce. The contract was then kept at the temple.

Sometimes a trial marriage was agreed upon, to see whether the wife or husband was fertile, and it was sometimes stipulated in the prenuptial contract that the marriage would end if pregnancy did not ensue within a year. Though the Egyptians have left no records of a formal marriage ceremony, it is known that they held a wedding party with the bride probably dressed in her best linen tunic and finest jewelry. Then the bride moved to her husband's house, taking all her belongings with her.

If you want an Egyptian theme for your handfasting, you might wear tunics of pleated linen and wigs, as the Egyptians did for social occasions. The place of ritual should be purified with incense. A sistrum rattle may be shaken to announce the start of the ritual when all the celebrants are in place. The high priest might call upon Isis, the goddess associated with marriage, and her consort Osiris, or upon Hathor, the goddess of love, and her consort Horus. The recorder of the ritual might wear the mask of Thoth, the ibis-headed scribe of the gods.

Native American

Many Native American groups traditionally formalized marriage through gift exchanges between the families of the bride and groom. The bride's family would give "women's things," such as beadwork, baskets, cloth, and cooking utensils, while the groom's family would give "men's things," like knives, hides, guns, horses, and blankets.

Ancient Greece

In ancient Athens, the favorite month for marriage was *Gamelion,* or January, since it was sacred to Hera, the goddess of marriage. The celebrations preferably took place at the full moon. After a formal betrothal ceremony, which dealt with the legal aspects of the marriage, the wedding itself took place a few days later. The bride dedicated her childish toys and girl's tunic to Artemis, the maiden goddess, to show that her childhood was over. Then she dressed in her finest clothes and veil, and went down to a party gathered at her father's house where the groom and his best man, or *paranymphos,* were waiting. A lamb was eaten, and everyone shared a large flat cake of pounded sesame seeds roasted and mixed with honey.

Then at some point in the evening, the bride's mother handed her over to the groom, who took her away in his chariot. He and the best man sat on either side of her as they processed to his house singing the marriage song "Ho, Hymen! Ho, Hymen! Hymenæous! Io!" while onlookers wished them well. At the groom's house, they were showered with confetti, and the bride had to stop on the threshold to eat a quince, a symbol of fertility. While the groom's friends continued to party, the bride was led, still veiled, to the flower-bedecked bridal chamber, where she was joined by the groom.

Holland

The bride and groom sit on thrones under a canopy of evergreens as the guests take turns offering good wishes.

Hungary

The groom gives the bride a bag of coins, while she gives him either three or seven handkerchiefs.

Iran

During the ceremony, a canopy of cloth is held over the heads of the bridal couple by happily married women. The same women later scatter sugar over their heads for luck, scraped from decorated sugar cones called *kalehghand*.

Italy

A ribbon is tied across the front of the church door to symbolize the bonding of the couple. Confetti or sugared almonds are tossed at the bride and groom for luck and fertility.

Malaysia

The gifts that the groom gives to the bride are carried to her house in procession by children. Each wedding guest is given a decorated egg, a symbol of fertility.

Morocco

Five days before the wedding, the bride is painted with henna on her hands and feet, and adorned with jewels. After the wedding, she circles her new home three times.

Norway

The bride wears silver jewelry and a gold crown edged with small silver discs, the ringing of which frightens off evil spirits. Two small fir trees are planted on either side of the door to the couple's house until they have their first child.

Poland

Reception guests pin money to the bride's veil. To ensure luck, she has to drink a glass of wine without spilling a drop.

Puerto Rico

A doll is dressed in a replica of the bridal dress and placed at the top table at the reception or perched on top of the cake. Little favors called *capias* are attached to it. The bride and groom pin one of these to each of the guests.

Romania

Guests toss sweets and nuts at the new couple to wish them prosperity.

Russia

After the ceremony, the bride and groom race to stand on a white rug. It is believed that whoever stands on it first will be master of the household.

Spain

The groom gives thirteen coins to the bride, symbolizing his ability to support her. During the ceremony, she carries them in a special purse.

Sweden

The bride has a silver coin from her father in her left shoe, and a gold coin from her mother in her right.

Switzerland

After the vows are taken, the matron of honor sets fire to the bridal wreath (which symbolizes the bride's virginity), and it is lucky if it burns quickly. A pine tree, symbolizing longevity and fertility, is planted at the couple's home.

Thailand

An older couple prepare the bridal bed with fertility symbols such as rice, sesame seeds, coins, and a cat.

Ukraine

A mock capture of the bride is carried out at the wedding.

Vietnam

The mother of a Vietnamese groom visits the bride's home on the wedding day to deliver betel and pink chalk (to symbolize a rosy future).

Yemen

The wedding feast is prepared by the bride's relatives and includes small sweet fritters, which symbolize a sweet life for the newlyweds. It is the duty of all the guests to play music and sing for the bride and groom.

1. Gunnora Hallakarva, "Courtship, Love and Marriage in Viking Scandinavia," http://www.drizzle.com/~celyn/mrwp/vikwed5.txt.

2. Edward Dwelly, *Gaelic Dictionary* (Herne Bay, England: E. MacDonald & Co., 1902).

3. Malcolm MacLennan, *Gaelic Dictionary* (1925; reprint, Aberdeen University Press, 1979).

4. Lady Wilde, *Ancient Legends, Mystic Charms, and Superstitions of Ireland* (Boston, MA: Ticknor and Co., 1887).

Chapter 7

HANDFASTING CUSTOMS

*I*n the past, weddings were seen as a time when people were particularly susceptible to bad luck and jealous evil spirits. In consequence, there are many customs and superstitions associated with weddings that originated centuries ago. They are maintained in the belief that they bring good luck and happiness to the couple at a time when their lives are on the point of change—hopefully for the better.

Tying the Knot

"Tying the knot," "getting hitched," and "joining hands in marriage" are common terms for getting married that originated in the handfasting custom of tying the couple's hands together. Some covens just tie the right hands together. A more modern custom is to tie right hand to right hand and left hand to left hand to make an infinity symbol (like a figure eight). It is considered that as the hands are bound together, so the couple are joined in love, trust, and mutual support.

Some covens allow the knots to be untied after the ceremony, while others insist that the couple remain bound for twenty-four hours so that they realize the serious nature of the commitment and just what is entailed in doing everything together. Don't worry, it can be great fun!

Jumping the Broom

When I was a child, people who lived together without being married were spoken of as "living over the brush." This referred to an old custom that meant a man and woman who wanted to live together could jump together over a broomstick and then be considered as common-law husband and wife. The old people maintained that this was a frequent practice among the Irish navvies (or "navigators") who came to England to help dig the canal networks and build the roads.

The broom, or *besom,* was associated with the marriage rite in Britain for hundreds of years. One English custom was that, at the reception, the groom would hold the broomstick parallel to the floor, and all the young men would rush across the room in an attempt to be the first to grasp the handle; he would be the next to marry.

European gypsies also jumped the broom as part of the marriage ceremony. African slaves in America adopted the custom when they had the right to marry taken away from them. The custom still features in some African-American weddings as a recognition of their heritage. German immigrant brides were thrown over the broom by unmarried girls in Pennsylvania.

The broom is a symbol of fertility, with the handle representing the male (an obvious phallic symbol) and the brush the female, a suitable emblem of a union between a man and a woman. The handle is usually made from a male wood, and the brush from a female tree or shrub. It is used to sweep the circle in an act of ritual purification and stands for the security of the hearth and home. It is an old fertility symbol, and in days past, the women would ride them around the fields, leaping as high as they could on them. The higher they leapt, the higher the crops would grow.

Traditionally, the witches' besom is made of an ash stake with birch twigs and an osier (willow) binding. The birch is for the expulsion of evil spirits, the ash is for protection and rebirth, and the willow is in homage to the Moon Goddess. However, the following are some alternate woods that you might prefer to use when making a broom.

Alder

Alder is used for support, for magical beginnings, and in fire and water magic. It is a male wood used for the handle of the broom.

Apple

An apple wand is used in love magic, rituals designed to establish contact with the Otherworld, initiations, and fertility rituals. Apple is a female wood; use the twigs for the brush of the broom.

Ash

The ash is a great conductor of magical force and is traditionally used for witches' broomsticks, druids' wands, and cunning men's staffs. The use of the ash wand connects the magician to the three realms of above, below, and middle earth. Ash is a male wood used for the handle of the broom.

Aspen

The aspen is used to invoke magical shields and for protection and healing. It is a male wood used for the handle of the broom.

Birch

The birch is a tree of fertility, but is also a powerful magical force in rituals of purification and the banishment of negativity. Birch is a female wood used for the brush of the broom.

Elder

The elder is used in rites of the crone goddess, in rites of Samhain and winter, and for fairy contact, healing, and summoning spirits. It is a female wood used for the brush of the broom.

Elm

The elm is used in rites of the Goddess and in feminine magic. It is a feminine wood used for the brush of the broom.

Hawthorn

Hawthorn is a female wood used for protection, for invoking a psychic shield, and for fairy contact. It is also used during the Beltane rituals and for summer Goddess magic.

Hazel

Hazel is a good general-purpose wand, some say the most efficacious of all wands. A hazel wand is sometimes called the wishing rod. It is a male wood used for the handle of the broom.

Holly

Holly is used in rites of male magic, in warrior magic, and for protection from negative forces. It is a male wood used for the handle of the broom.

Ivy

Ivy is a female wood used in binding magic and for protection from psychic attack. It may be used to fasten the twigs of the broom to the shaft.

Linden

Linden is used for feminine power and in rites of the Goddess. It is a female wood used for the brush of the broom.

Maple

Maple is a male wood that promotes enthusiasm and energy in relationships.

Oak

Oak is used in rites of protection, for general-purpose magic, at Midsummer, and for divination, fairy contact, and Otherworld magic. It is a male wood used for the handle of the broom.

Rowan

Rowan is used for protection and divination. It is a female wood used for the brush of the broom.

Spindle Tree

The spindle tree is used for spinning and weaving magic, creation magic, and Goddess magic. It is a female wood used for the brush of the broom.

Willow

Willow is a female wood used for Bardic magic, healing, Goddess magic, feminine magic, rites of rebirth and purification. Willow withies are used for binding the broom.

The handfasted couple usually jump the broom after the ceremony. Two people hold the broom at a convenient height so that the bride and groom can jump over it, hand in hand, taking a leap into the future. Sometimes they are told that they must leap over it once for each child they wish to have, while others simply leap over it three times.

Jumping the Cauldron

An alternative to the fertility ritual of jumping the broomstick is to jump the cauldron. A cauldron is essentially a cooking pot, a vessel that transforms raw ingredients into something new. There are many cauldrons in Celtic myth, owned by various gods and goddesses.

Some magically produce sustenance, some transform, some hold the fruits of the harvest, and others bring the dead to life. In essence, all of these cauldrons represent the womb of the Goddess, which transforms everything that is laid within it. The cauldron is a symbol of initiation, renewal, rebirth, and plenty. It may contain water, fire, incense, or flowers, as the occasion demands.

It is nice to fill the cauldron with water and float suitable flowers and herbs on the surface:

Apple *Malus sp.*

Apple blossom is associated with the goddess of fertility, lust, love, and marriage. When an apple is cut in half, it reveals a pentacle, the symbol of the goddess and the planet Venus, ruler of love.

Basil *Ocimum sp.*

Basil is called the *Witch's Herb,* and throughout the ages witches have employed it in various forms of magic—for healing and revitalizing the body and in love spells.

Daisy (English) *Bellis perennis*

The daisy is associated with purity, innocence, and faithful love.

Marigold *Calendula officinalis*

Marigold is used for healing, protection, love, and divination.

Marjoram *Origanum vulgare*

Marjoram is sacred to the Goddess of Love, and may be used to invoke her in all her aspects.

Meadowsweet *Filipendula ulmaria/Spiraea ulmaria*

Meadowsweet is sacred to Aine, Blodeuwedd, Gwena, and Venus. Use this herb for love, marriage and handfasting, fertility, and abundance.

Myrrh *Commiphora myrrha*

Myrrh is used for spells and rituals of handfasting, love, fertility, death, regeneration, and rebirth. It is sacred to Adonis, Demeter, Freya, Hathor, Hecate, Hera, Isis, Juno, Marian, Mut, Aphrodite, and Dionysus.

Myrtle *Myrtus communis*

Myrtle is dedicated to the planet Venus and the Moon, and is sacred to Aphrodite, Artemis, Astarte, Ashtoreth, Freya, Hathor, Marian, Venus, Myrrha, Thetis, the Graces, and Hera. It is a tree that reflects the Goddess in all her aspects, and is employed for prophecy, love, fertility, and marriage.

Primrose *Primula vulgaris*

The primrose attracts love and glamour, and is sacred to Freya and Blodeuwedd and all goddesses of the spring and love.

Rose *Rosa sp.*

Red roses are ruled by Jupiter, damask roses by the planet Venus, and white roses by the Moon. The white rose represents purity, perfection, innocence, virginity, and the Maiden Goddess, while the red rose is earthly passion and fertility, the Mother Goddess. Use rose petals for spells and rituals of love, passion, sexuality, sensuality, seduction, marriage, the Great Rite, and handfasting.

Rosemary *Rosemarinus officinalis*

Rosemary is used for healing, marriage, to keep a lover faithful, and for love spells.

Violet (Sweet) *Viola odorata*

Violet is a symbol of fertility and is frequently added to love potions. Mix it with lavender to attract a new love. Violet is a symbol of the constancy of love and fertility, and is sacred to Aphrodite, Venus, and other goddesses of love.

Sharing a Cup

The couple may wish to share a cup of wine as part of the formal procedure. Special loving cups with two handles are employed in some countries, or the cup can be a simple goblet or glass. Drinking from the same cup is a token that the couple will share everything from then on. Sometimes it is broken afterward as a sign that no one else shall share what they have.

Throwing the Bouquet

Throwing the bouquet may be a very old practice dating back to Pagan times. The bride tosses the bouquet over her head to the unmarried women who cluster behind her. The one who catches it will be the next to marry.

Showering with Rice and Confetti

In ages past, it was the convention to shower the bride and groom with rice, grains, nuts, flower petals, and sweets, partly as an act of sympathetic magic so they would never go hungry, and partly as an invocation of fertility, represented by these items. Unmarried women often scrambled to pick up the grains so that the luck would rub off, and they too would find a mate.

Today, confetti made from colored paper is often thrown by the wedding party after the ceremony. In Italy, confetti were originally little sweets that were sprinkled on the happy couple to indicate that their life together would be sweet. In some places, the wedding cake was not eaten, but thrown at the bride!

Be wary of using rice, which can be hazardous for any birds that eat it. Flower petals are a nice alternative, but can become slippery if too many are used. (The Victorians introduced the idea of a flower girl who strews the path of the bride and groom with blossoms.) If you use paper confetti, make sure it is environmentally friendly.

Shoes

Shoes play a part in weddings in many parts of the world. We are familiar with the tying of old shoes on the back of the wedding car for good fortune, but in the Tudor period, the shoes would actually have been thrown at the bride and groom, and the luck was transferred if they were actually hit.

Another ancient custom, practiced by both the ancient Egyptians and Anglo-Saxons, was the passing over of a pair of the bride's slippers by her father to the groom, to symbolize the passing of authority from one to the other. The groom then tapped her on the head with one of the slippers to indicate his dominance. Imagine a modern woman putting up with that!

Rather than throwing her bouquet over her shoulder, the German bride threw a slipper. Whoever caught it would be the next to marry.

The Honeymoon

The idea of the honeymoon comes from the ancient Teutonic people. The bride and groom kept their own company and drank honey wine for a full month, or moon, after the wedding, so this became known as the honey moon period. Honey was widely believed to be an aphrodisiac in ancient and medieval times. It was an indispensable ingredient of love potions and spells or was taken with food and wine. Nowadays, the honeymoon is a special holiday away from everything for the newly married couple.

The Cake

The wedding cake probably originated with the ancient Romans, who baked small wheat or barley cakes and broke them over the bride's head as an act of fertility magic. Around 100 BCE, they began creating small, sweet cakes that were eaten while the ritual was conducted. The custom seems to have spread throughout Europe in the centuries that followed. In the Middle Ages in Britain, small flat cakes containing fruit and nuts were piled up into a mound, the taller the better, and the bride and groom had to kiss over the top of it for good luck. After the wedding, any leftovers were distributed among the poor. It was during the reign of Charles II of England that the cake was first iced when a visiting French chef decided to improve on the cake mound custom. Today's usual three-tier wedding cake is said to be an imitation of the unusual spire of Saint Bride's Church in London. Such a cake was first baked for the wedding of Queen Victoria's daughter in 1859. It wasn't until the marriage of Prince Leopold in 1882 that the supporting pillars were added.

The bride and groom make the first cut together as yet another mark that they will share everything. Every guest is given a slice, and those relatives and friends who are unable to attend the reception are sent a piece for good fortune. The top tier of the cake is often kept by couples for the christening of their first child.

A number of spells were customarily performed with wedding cake, such as this traditional one, whereby a woman slept with a piece of cake beneath her pillow to help her dream of her future husband:

But madam, as a present take
This little paper of bride-cake;
Fast any Friday in the year,
When Venus mounts the starry sphere,
Thrust this at night in pillowbeer:
In morning slumber you will seem
T' enjoy your lover in a dream.

In Yorkshire, a plate holding wedding cake was thrown out of the window as the bride returned to her parental home after the wedding. If the plate broke, she would enjoy a happy future with her husband, but if the plate remained intact, her prospects would be grim.

Another old English custom was to place a ring in the wedding cake. The guest who found it in their piece of cake would be ensured happiness for the next year. In the 1700s it became the tradition to push a small piece of the cake through the wedding ring a certain number of times (nine being the usual number), and sleep with it beneath the pillow for luck.

As a Pagan you might consider the relevance of the number three and the three tiers of the cake. Three is a sacred number of the Goddess and refers to her triple aspects as Maiden, Mother, and Crone. You can choose the colors of the icing and any decorations to reflect your personal beliefs and needs.

Bride Ale

In medieval England, the tradition broadened to include the practice of washing down the cakes with a special ale called *bryd ealu,* or "bride's ale," words that eventually became the word *bridal.* (See also the handfasting recipes in chapter 10.)

Flowers

Flowers have played a part in weddings since the earliest times. They represent sweetness, beauty, joy, and fecundity. They are employed today in the form of buttonholes, corsages, bouquets, posies, wreaths, and table arrangements. (For more information on flowers and handfastings, see chapter 9 on handfasting herb craft.)

Nuts

Nuts are an obvious fertility symbol. They were once thrown at the bridal couple in place of rice or confetti. Guest favors often take the form of almonds.

Unity Candle

Here is a simple ritual that is used by people of many different faiths as a symbol of joining. It utilizes three candles. The outer two represent the bride and groom as individuals. They each lift their candle and use it to light the central, larger candle, as a symbol that what was once two has become one and cannot be separated. The side candles are then extinguished or left burning, as desired.

Wishing Well

If the wedding takes place near a well, river, or stream, the guests can throw coins into the water, invoking the water spirits to bless the couple.

Eggs

A natural symbol of fertility and promise, the egg features in many wedding customs. Sometimes eggs were thrown at the bride and groom (I presume they were hard-boiled first), and sometimes they were painted and given to the couple or guests as gifts. In Ireland, a laying hen was tied to the bed on the first honeymoon night in the hope that it would lay an egg, which would be a fortuitous omen. Eating a double-yolked egg was also thought to bring fecundity.

Roses

The red rose is a symbol of love and passion, and is sacred to the Goddess of Love. You can present your beloved with a single red rose after taking your vows, as the first gift of your married life.

The Hen Night or Bridal Shower

The hen night is held a night or two before the wedding for the bride and her friends to mark the last hours of being single. In Britain, this generally takes the form of a lively evening out on the town. In my own home town of Hinckley, the factory girls had a custom that seems to be peculiar to the district. During her lunch break on her last day as a single woman, the prospective bride was taken out and dressed in an elaborate hat made from paper flowers by her workmates, and tied to a lamppost. The lamppost is probably just a more modern joke, but the flowered headdress may date back to old fertility customs.

In the United States, a bridal shower is more usual, when the bride and her friends get together to open gifts and prepare for the wedding.

Pagan women may organize the evening a little differently, and spend the time making women's magic or telling women's stories over food and wine.

The Stag Night or Bachelor Party

While the women hold their hen night, the groom and his friends hold a stag party. In Europe, this term was once quite literal, when the man had to prove his virility by running with and hunting a stag. Ancient Spartan soldiers are thought to have been among the first to hold bachelor parties. The groom feasted with his comrades on the night before the wedding, swearing eternal friendship with them and saying farewell to his bachelor days.

Pagan men may go back to the roots of the tradition, and hold games and contests of skill, drink mead from the drinking horn, and tell boastful stories of male prowess.

Wedding Favors

Pieces of the bride's attire were considered very lucky, and guests tried to steal them to take home; desperate brides resorted to sewing ribbons onto their dresses. This eventually evolved into the practice of giving wedding favors to the guests. In Italy, guests are given little bags of sweets, usually sugared almonds. Favors might include nosegays of herbs or flowers, packets of seeds, or chocolates.

Chapter 8

WHAT TO WEAR

$\mathcal{W}$e already discussed some clothing options for various wedding themes in chapter 6. This chapter contains some general advice on ritual clothing for handfastings.

The Wedding Dress in History

Bridal apparel has always been a matter of deep concern. What the bride wore might make good or bad magic for her subsequent life. We often associate the color white with the wedding dress, but historically brides wore dresses of many different shades. Ancient Greek and Roman brides wore white to ward off evil spirits and to symbolize purity and innocence, but it was not often worn in Christian countries until the Middle Ages, when Anne of Brittany wore one at her wedding in 1499. There is not another mention of this until 1530 when the daughter of Henry VII, Margaret Tudor, married James IV of Scotland. Both bride and groom wore white damask, edged and lined in crimson velvet. Until the Victorian era, girls usually just wore their best clothes until Queen Victoria herself made white fashionable by wearing it for her marriage to Prince Albert in 1840. However, there were various superstitions as to which colors were most suitable for a bride.

A traditional Victorian verse states:

Married in grey, you will go far away,
Married in red, you will wish yourself dead,
Married in green, ashamed to be seen,
Married in blue, your love will be true,
Married in pearl, you will live in a whirl,
Married in yellow, ashamed of your fellow,
Married in brown, you will live in a town,
Married in pink, your spirit will sink,
Married in black, you will wish yourself back.

Green was considered particularly bad because to say a girl had a green dress implied that she had been rolling about on the grass with a lover. In Ireland, it was considered particularly unlucky as it was deemed the fairies' color, and taboo for humans. The idea of the Irish bride in emerald green is a very modern one. In China, the color of love and luck is red, so it is chosen for the bride's dress and the money envelopes that are presented to her. In Japan, white was always the color of choice for bridal clothing, while Korean brides wear bright reds and yellows.

Other superstitions state that the bride should never make her own dress, that the final stitch should not be completed until she is departing for the ceremony, and that she should never try on the complete outfit before the day of the wedding, or mark the linen with her married name. This was thought to tempt fate by "counting her chickens before they were hatched," so to speak.

Color Magic

You probably have your own favorite shades and a personal prefer-ence for colors in clothes and decor, but color may have more of an influence on you than you realize. The seven colors of light are demonstrated when a prism breaks up white light into its component parts. Light is an electromagnetic energy produced by the sun in differing wavelengths. We perceive these as different colors. At either end of the visible spectrum are ultraviolet and infrared wavelengths, not visible to us, but affecting us just the same. In the occult and in healing, colors are also seen as having a certain vibration, or wavelength. Six of the seven chakra colors are six of the colors of the rainbow, the visible spectrum of light, while the crown chakra is white and contains the potential of all the others. Red is a low light vibration, activating the root chakra, producing feelings of strength, passion, etc. At the other end of the scale, violet is a high vibration color, which activates the third eye chakra, producing feelings of inspiration, dream activity, and spirituality.

There is plenty of Pagan lore about colors, and you might like to consider the following before designing your outfits.

Red

Red is deeply linked with the supernatural. It is the color of witchcraft; in fairy tales witches often wear red cloaks, have red hair, or wear red caps. According to W. B. Yeats, Irish witches put little red caps on their heads before flying off to the Sabbats. Old Mother Redcap was a generic name for a witch or wise-woman in England.

As the color of blood, red is the color of life, passion, lust, vitality, completion, and harvest. Red represents influence and authority; red carpets are still unrolled for VIPs. It is a powerful color, emblematic of fire, and as such is protective, and effective against psychic attack.

Green

Green is very much associated with fairies. They are often described as wearing green clothes, coats, and caps. Some even have green skin. In Ireland, green is so much the fairy color that it was considered (until very recent times) unlucky for humans to wear it, while in Scotland, any woman dressed in green was sure to be a fairy.

Green is also described as the color of envy. This may be because it is a color of the gods and spirits. Whatever the origin of the belief, the correspondence of green and envy has passed into folk custom. In Scotland, if a girl married before her older sister, she had to give her a present of green stockings. In England, an unmarried older sister had to dance at her younger sister's wedding wearing green stockings.

In contrast, modern pagans wear green to symbolize fertility, prosperity, growth, creativity, love, change, and balance.

Black

Black is the color of darkness and night, and is linked with the planet Saturn, death, and dissolution. Alternatively, it encompasses the rejection of ego, possibilities waiting to be realized, anticipation, strength, empowerment, and wisdom. Witches often wear black robes.

Blue

Blue is the color of the sky, and is associated with the planet Jupiter and with various goddesses, especially Queens of Heaven such as Juno and Hera. It is the color of eternity, purity, faith, modesty, tranquillity, healing, spiritual development, protection, and calm.

Brown

Brown is the color of earthiness, sexuality, practicality, the home, and environmental awareness.

Gold

Gold symbolizes spiritual strength, spiritual zest, the sun, healing, wealth, divination, knowledge, the Sun God, and service to others.

Gray

Gray connects with the planet Mercury and communication of all kinds.

Indigo

Indigo is emblematic of perceptiveness, vision, longevity, and intuition.

Magenta

Magenta is the color of vision, creativity, and insight.

Orange

Orange relates to optimism, success, courage, bravery, and ambition.

Pink

Pink is the color of love, friendship, happiness, harmony, peace, romance, and compassion.

Purple

Purple represents strength, mastery, and occult power.

Silver

Silver is the color of the moon and the Moon Goddess, intuition, truth, enlightenment, poetry, and inspiration.

Turquoise

Turquoise represents inventiveness, conception, and philosophy.

Violet

Violet is the color of mastery, ceremony, self-respect, spiritual growth, and fulfillment.

Yellow

Yellow relates to the element of air, sound and speech, intellectual development, and strength of mind.

The Veil

Ancient Greeks and Romans thought the veil protected the bride from evil spirits. Brides have worn veils ever since. The veil became popular in Britain in the 1800s as a symbol of modesty and chastity.

In some Eastern countries where the marriage is arranged, the bride and groom do not see each other until the ceremony is over and the veil is lifted from the bride's face.

The Garter

Western brides wear garters beneath their dresses. One may be thrown to the bachelors as the bouquet is thrown to the unmarried girls. The removal of the garter by the groom has a sexual connotation, and used to demonstrate the leaving behind of the virginal state.

The Handfast Cord

Cords are very much associated with witches, who wear and keep them for spell casting by knotting them in various ways. The use of knots in magic is very old, with their implications of tying and binding, untying and releasing. Some of the magical implications of knot magic still survive in the English language where people speak of marriage as "tying the knot." In the marriage customs of some parts of the world, the couple's hands are actually tied together to symbolize this, just as they are in the Wiccan ceremony of handfasting. When we part from someone, we may speak of "severing the bond." And, of course, the very first knot we all experience is the knot in the umbilical cord.

In ancient Egypt, the knot was a symbol of the goddess Isis, usually depicted as a knotted cloth between her breasts. Ancient Romans were so in fear of the power of the knot to bind and limit energies that the high priest, the *Flamen Dialis,* was forbidden to wear any knot or closed ring on his person, in case it bound up his powers.

The cords used to bind the couple's hands together in the handfasting ceremony should be made from a natural material such as cotton, wool, or silk. You can plait different colors together to symbolize the weaving and joining of different forces and concepts. In length it should be some multiple of three: three feet, six inches, nine inches, nine centimeters, etc.

The Rings

Pagans often choose to exchange rings during the handfasting. Though it is not traditionally part of the service, it is customary in most parts of the modern world and a nice demonstration of commitment. The rings are placed on the Book of Shadows or the pentacle and blessed by the celebrant. The bride and groom then place them on each other's third finger of the left hand with words such as: "This ring is the symbol of wholeness and perfection. It is a token of my love." You might like to follow a medieval tradition and slip the ring onto three fingers in turn, saying: "In the name of the Maiden, in the name of the Mother, and in the name of the Crone, I give you this ring in token of my love and commitment."

The idea of the wedding ring dates back to ancient times, when a coin or ring would be split, with the bride receiving half and the groom half, to demonstrate that they were two halves of one whole. When someone wears a wedding ring, it is an announcement to the world that they are married, part of a loving couple. It is a public symbol of a private commitment and a constant reminder of the pledges made on the handfasting or wedding day. There was an ancient Roman belief that a vein ran from the fourth finger of the left hand directly to the heart, and that placing a wedding ring on this finger ensured the faithfulness of the heart. Today, many divorced people remove their wedding rings, but it was once the case that widows and widowers were expected to remove their rings to show that they were no longer married.

For Pagans, the ring also stands for the magic circle that guards the sacred rites of the Craft, and which stands for the wholeness of creation. The ring is an ancient symbol of wholeness, unity, and perfection, a thing without beginning or end. Therefore the exchanging of rings is a magical act and a sacred oath before the gods.

Types of Rings

While many people use plain gold bands as wedding rings, this was not always the case. Mary Queen of Scots sent a diamond ring to Thomas, Duke of Norfolk, as a symbol of her willingness to marry him. Margaret Audley, the Duchess of Norfolk, was shown with a large diamond on the third finger of her left hand.

Pagans are not limited to a single style of ring, and may choose something much more personal, perhaps using Goddess metals such as copper or silver instead of the usual gold. They may choose designs that have meaning for them such as pentacles, moons, gods and goddesses, hearts, ankhs, and so on. I wear a silver ring with the three phases of the moon, with silver crescents of the waxing and waning moons set on each side of a full moon made by a round moonstone.

The Serpent Ring

Snake rings dotted with ruby eyes were popular wedding rings in Victorian England, with the coils winding into a circle symbolizing eternity. The serpent is a powerful Pagan symbol of regeneration, renewal, and infinity.

Clasped Hands

A pair of gold rings was exchanged by Admiral Lord Nelson and his mistress, Lady Emma Hamilton, in the seventeenth century. They took the form of clasped hands, as a symbol of love. Nelson's ring is now kept at the National Maritime Museum at Greenwich in London.

The Claddagh Ring

This Irish design is used by many Celtic Pagans. It takes the form of a hand, a heart, and a crown, signifying faith, love, and loyalty.

The Poesy Ring

This ring consists of from three to eight interlocking bands, each bearing a line of verse or a word, which create a poem or motto. For example:

> *How do I love thee?*
> *Let me count the ways*
> *I love thee to the depth*
> *And breadth and height*
> *For the ends of Being*
> *And ideal Grace.*

Some versions open to reveal a little heart.

The Puzzle Ring

This ring consists of interlocking pieces that fall apart when the ring is taken off. According to one story, it was invented by a sultan who wished to assure himself of his wife's constancy. He knew that she would remove her wedding ring if ever she committed adultery and would not be able to reassemble it.

Inscriptions on the Rings

A nice old custom is to have the rings engraved, usually in French or Latin.

> *Nemo nisi mors* (Till death divide)
>
> *True Love*
>
> *Forever*
>
> *Deux corps un coeur* (Two bodies one heart)

With everlasting love

I am yours

Semper Amenus (May we love forever)

Love me truly

Tout pour bien feyre (In good faith)

After consent, ever content

Love me and leave me not

In perfect love and perfect trust

Amot vincit om (Love conquers all)

Mon coeur avez (You have my heart)

Using Gemstones in the Rings

If your rings are to be set with gemstones, it is worthwhile making sure these are suitable for the purpose. Here is a list of gemstones and how they relate to love and marriage.

Agate

Agate attracts good friends. It is particularly good for Geminis, but should not be worn by Pisceans or Virgos.

Alexandrite

Alexandrite ensures luck in love.

Amazonite

Amazonite increases courage and improves a woman's success in love.

Amber

Amber is not a stone, but a translucent fossil tree resin formed millions of years ago. It is pale yellow or brownish in color, often with plants and insects trapped within. The Norse believed that amber was the tears of the love goddess Freya, shed into the sea when her husband Odur (the summer sun) left her in the winter. Amber is particularly good for Leos.

Amethyst

Amethyst comes from the Greek *amethystos,* meaning "not intoxicating." If a man wears it, good women will love him. Amethyst brings luck and ensures constancy, and is especially good for Pisceans.

Apache Tear Drop

Apache tear drops are lucky. It is said that those who possess one of the stones will never have to shed tears again.

Aquamarine

Aquamarine represents marital harmony and is said to promote a long and happy marriage. It helps attract a soul mate, and ensures constancy in a new bride.

Aventurine

Aventurine brings luck in love.

Beryl

Beryl brings about love and harmony between married couples.

Blue Quartz

Blue quartz may be worn by a man to attract a soul mate.

Carnelian

Carnelian (also called cornelian) helps both men and women attract a soul mate. It also increases sexual desire.

Chalcedony

Those who wear chalcedony will be lucky in law and love, energetic, strong, and free of melancholy, illusion, and evil spirits.

Chrysophase

Chrysophase enhances luck in love and helps mend a broken heart. It improves a man's success in love. Chrysophase should not be worn by Virgos or Pisceans.

Citrine

Citrine increases feelings of self-worth and self-confidence, especially in women. It can be used to infuse new life into a relationship that has gone stale. It is especially good for Geminis.

Coral

Coral, usually yellowish red or pink, is made from the skeletons of certain marine animals and is not a true gemstone. It helps you think and behave in a loving manner.

Diamond

Set in gold and silver, diamonds have been a popular choice for wedding and engagement rings since the fifteenth century. The Venetians believed that the diamond was created from the flames of love. The diamond is a talisman for reconciling husbands and wives who have quarreled. It intensifies the properties of gems with which it is set, particularly amethysts and emeralds. Diamond is a symbol of eternal love.

Emerald

Emerald helps revive a stale romantic relationship.

Garnet

Garnet secures love. It is especially attractive to Leos.

Haematite

Haematite (also called hematite) increases self-confidence and self-esteem.

Hag Stone

Hag stones are small pebbles that have natural holes in them. They are excellent amulets against disease and the evil eye. Those shaped like a couple embracing (you really have to use your imagination for this) are charms to bring love.

Jacinth

Deep yellow jacinth may be taken in a potion to drive away melancholy. This is prepared by putting the gem in spring water in a clear glass jar and leaving it in sunlight for three days. Given to another, the potion or the stone will win his or her affection. Jacinths are particularly beneficial for Aquarians.

Jade

Jade (also called Jadeite or Nephrite) attracts love (particularly that of an Aquarian) and prosperity. Jade butterflies symbolize love at Chinese weddings.

Kunzite

Kunzite attracts love, and is often used in love spells.

Kyanite

Kyanite attracts love. Give this gemstone to a Taurean or Aries to secure their love.

Lepidolite

Lepidolite improves openness and trust.

Loadstone

Loadstone (also called lodestone) was used in medieval times as a test of faithfulness. It was said that if a lodestone was laid under the head of a virtuous woman as she slept, she would turn and embrace her husband. If she was unfaithful, she would fall out of bed!

Worn as an amulet, lodestone reconciles lovers' quarrels, though it should never be used by Leos or Aquarians. Lodestone increases sexual desire and virility.

Malachite

Malachite contains a great deal of copper (sacred to Venus, the goddess of love), which makes it green. It helps both men and women attract a soul mate.

Moonstone

Moonstone is receptive, and helps balance and soothe the emotions. It helps a woman attract a soul mate. If a man gives his woman a moonstone, it will ensure her continued interest. Sacred to Venus, the goddess of love, moonstone is often used as a love amulet.

Opal

The opal is sacred to Venus, Roman goddess of love. It is said that if an opal wearer deceives another in love, or abuses a lover, the stone will bring the wearer bad luck.

Pearl

The pearl is considered unlucky in a wedding or engagement ring as the shape looks like a tear, and thus the pearl is thought to bring tears. The exception is for those born under the sign of Cancer. Give a pearl to a Cancerian to secure their love.

Pink Calcite

Pink calcite helps foster feelings of love.

Quartz

Quartz enhances the properties of other gemstones.

Rhodonite

Rhodonite attracts love.

Rose Quartz

Rose quartz brings sleep, calms the emotions, and eases the heart of traumas and leaves it open to love. This gemstone replaces resentment with inner peace, and is often used in love spells. It promotes vibrations of universal love and enlivens the imagination. Rose quartz channels love energy and improves a woman's success in love.

Ruby

Ruby excites sexuality, invigorates the root chakra, and strengthens a good relationship but splits apart a bad one. It helps foster feelings of love and passion. Ruby is good for Capricorns, but should be avoided by Aries and Librans.

Ruby Zoisite

Ruby zoisite increases sexual desire.

Sapphire

Set in a wedding ring, sapphire is said to bring marital happiness. You should not buy a sapphire for yourself, but it should always be a gift. If a man gives his woman a sapphire, it will ensure her continued interest in him.

Smokey Quartz

Smokey quartz improves a man's success in love and increases courage.

Spinal

Spinal promotes sexual energy and desire. It is good for Capricorns.

Sunstone

Sunstone improves luck in love.

Tourmaline

Tourmalines come in many hues, from black, through green, pink, yellow, blue, white, and red; a rare variety contains three different shades in its makeup. All of the colors attract love and friendship. Though the red stone is the most powerful in general, you might give a watermelon tourmaline to a Gemini or Virgo to secure their love, a dark pink tourmaline to a Scorpio or Sagittarian, a green tourmaline to a Capricorn, and light pink tourmaline to a Libran.

Turquoise

Turquoise is known as the stone of Venus (the planet of love) and it helps foster feelings of love and affection. It may help reconcile a husband and wife who have quarreled. It is especially lucky for Taureans and Sagittarians. The qualities of the gem are enhanced by being set in silver.

Unikite

Unikite awakens love in the heart chakra and helps balance the emotions.

Yellow Zircon

Yellow zircon attracts love into your life.

Chapter 9

HANDFASTING
HERB CRAFT

$\mathcal{U}$sing flowers and herbs at weddings is an ancient custom. There are many ways to use flowers and herbs at a handfasting:

- In the incense
- As confetti
- Circle decorations
- Room decorations
- Altar decorations
- The bridal bouquet
- The maid's bouquets
- In baskets of flowers to be carried or for decoration
- In wreaths and chaplets for bride, groom, maids, and grooms-men, and even for all the guests, if you wish
- Buttonholes for the guests
- Nosegays or posies for the guests

- For strewing
- In food and drink, including the Lovers' Cup
- In potions and spells
- In consecration oils and decoctions

The Victorian Language of Flowers

The Victorians popularized the use of flower symbolism for sending messages in the formalized "language of flowers." For example, if a man wanted to tell a woman that he loved only her, he would send her a cedar leaf. If she wasn't interested, she might respond with burdock, meaning "touch me not." If his feelings were returned, she might respond with shepherd's purse, meaning "I give thee my all." The practice was extended to use in the bridal bouquet, in which carefully chosen flowers might express constancy (bluebell), fidelity (ivy), and so on. The first real floral "dictionary" was published in 1818, but others followed and some disagreed on meanings, which meant that the giver and receiver were sometimes at cross-purposes!

Acacia: Friendship, chaste love

Acanthus: Artifice

Adonis: Bitter memories

Agnus castus: Coldness, indifference

Agrimony: Gratitude

Allspice: Compassion

Almond: Hope

Aloe: Sorrow, dejection

Althea: Consumed by love

Alyssum, sweet: Worth beyond beauty

Amaranth: Unfading love

Amaryllis: Splendid beauty

Anemone (garden): Forsaken

Anemone (wild): Anticipation

Angelica: Inspiration

Apple blossom: Preference

Arbour vitae: Unchanging friendship

Arbutus: Thee only do I love

Arum (cuckoo pint): Ardor

Ash: Grandeur

Aspen: Lamentation

Asphodel: Remembered beyond the grave

Aster: Variety

Auricular, red: Avarice

Autumn crocus: Do not abuse me

Azalea: Romance

Balm of gilead: Relief

Balm: Sympathy

Balsam: Impatience

Barberry: Sourness of temper

Basil: Give me your good wishes

Bay: I will not change till death

Bee orchid: Error

Beech: Lover's tryst

Belladonna: Silence

Betony: Surprise

Bilberry: Treachery

Bindweed: Hopes extinguished

Birch: Meekness

Birdsfoot, trefoil: Revenge

Bittersweet: Truth

Black bryony: Be my support

Blackthorn: Difficulties

Bluebell: Constancy

Borage: Bluntness

Box: Constancy

Bramble: Remorse

Broom: Neatness

Buckbean: Calm repose

Bugloss: Falsehood

Burdock: Touch me not

Buttercup: Childishness

Cabbage: Profit

Cactus: Thou leavest me

Calla lily: Feminine beauty

Camellia, red: Unpretending excellence

Camellia, white: Perfected loveliness

Camomile: Energy in adversity

Candytuft: Indifference

Canterbury bell: Gratitude

Carnation: Pure and deep love

Carnation, striped: Refusal

Carnation, deep red: Alas for my heart!

Carnation, pink: Woman's love

Carnation, yellow: Disdain

Cedar leaf: I live for thee

Cedar of Lebanon: Incorruptible

Celandine, lesser: Joys to come

Centaury: Delicacy

Cereus, night blooming: Transient beauty

Cherry blossom: Spiritual beauty

Chickweed: Rendezvous

Christmas rose: Relieve my anxiety

Chrysanthemum, yellow: Slighted love

Chrysanthemum, red: I love

Chrysanthemum, white: Truth

Cinnamon: Forgiveness

Clover, four-leaf: Be mine

Clover, red: Industry

Clover, white: I promise

Cloves: Dignity

Cockle: Vain beauty is without merit

Colchicum: My best days have fled

Columbine: Desertion

Convolvulus: Bonds

Corcopsis: Love at first sight

Coreopsis: Always cheerful

Coriander: Hidden

Cowslip: Pensiveness

Cranberry: Cure for heartache

Cress: Stability

Crocus: Cheerfulness

Crowfoot: Ingratitude

Cucumber: Criticism

Currants: Thy frown will kill me

Cyclamen: Diffidence

Cypress: Despair

Daffodil: Regard, chivalry

Dahlia: Forever thine

Daisy, English: Innocence

Daisy, garden: I share your feelings

Daisy, Michaelmas: Farewell

Daisy, ox eye: Patience

Dandelion: Coquetry

Datura: Deceitful charms

Dead leaves: Sadness

Dittany of Crete: Birth

Dock: Patience

Dogbane: Deceit

Eglantine: I wound to heal

Elder: Compassion

Elecampane: Tears

Elm: Dignity

Endive: Frugality

Eupatorium: Delay

Evening primrose: Inconstancy

Fennel: Strength

Fern: Fascination

Fig: Argument

Filbert: Reconciliation

Fir: Elevation

Flax: I feel your kindness

Fleur-de-lis: I burn for thee

Forget-me-not: Do not forget me

Foxglove: Insincerity

Fritillary (crown imperial): Pride of birth

Fritillary (snakeshead): Persecution

Fuchsia: Humble love

Furze: Anger

Gardenia: Ecstasy

Gentian: Intrinsic worth

Geranium, ivy: Bridal favor

Gillyflower: Bonds of affection

Gladiolus: Ready-armed

Goat's rue: Reason

Goldenrod: Encouragement

Gooseberry: Anticipation

Goosefoot: Goodness

Grape: Charity

Grass: Submission

Guilder rose: Winter

Harebell: Grief

Hawthorn: Hope

Hazel: Reconciliation

Heartsease: You occupy my thoughts

Helenium: Tears

Heliotrope: Devotion, faithfulness

Hellebore: Scandal

Hemlock: You will be my death

Hibiscus: Delicate beauty

Holly: Am I forgotten?

Hollyhock: Fruitfulness

Honeysuckle: The bond of love

Hop: Injustice

Hornbeam: Ornament

Horse chestnut: Luxury

Hortensia: You are cold

House leek: Domestic economy

Hyacinth: Jealousy

Hydrangea: Heartlessness

Hyssop: Cleanliness

Ice plant: Your looks freeze me

Ipomaca: I attach myself to you

Iris: Message for you

Ivy: Fidelity, marriage

Jacob's ladder: Come down

Jasmine, cape: Transports of joy

Jasmine, Indian: I attach myself to you

Jasmine, white: Amiability

Jasmine, yellow: Grace and elegance

Jonquil: Return my affection

Judas tree: Betrayed

Juniper: Perfect loveliness

Kings-cup: I wish I were rich

Laburnum: Pensive beauty

Lady's slipper: Capricious beauty

Larch: Boldness

Larkspur: Fickleness

Lavatera: Sweet disposition

Lavender: Distrust

Lemon blossoms: Fidelity in love

Lettuce: Cold-hearted

Lichen: Dejected

Lilac: First emotion of love

Lily of the valley: Return of happiness

Lily, day: Coquetry

Lily, white: Purity, sweetness, modesty

Lily, yellow: Falsehood

Lime or linden tree: Conjugal love

Liverwort: Confidence

Locust tree: Affection beyond the grave

Loosestrife: Pretension

Lotus: Forgetful of the past

Love in a mist: You puzzle me

Love lies bleeding: Hopeless, not heartless

Lucerne: Life

Madder: Calumny

Magnolia: Love of nature

Maize: Riches

Mallow: Sweetness, kindness

Mandrake: Horror

Maple: Reserve

Marigold, African: Vulgar-minded

Marigold, French: Jealousy

Marigold, garden: Sacred affection

Marigold: Cruelty

Marjoram: Blushes

Marshmallow: Beneficence

Meadowsweet: Usefulness

Mignonette: Moral and mental beauty

Milkweed: Hope in misery

Mimosa: Sensitivity

Mint: Virtue

Mistletoe: I surmount all difficulties and obstacles

Mock orange: Counterfeit

Monkshood: A foe is near

Motherwort: Secret love

Mugwort: Happiness

Mulberry, white: Wisdom

Mulberry, black: I will not survive you

Mullein: Good nature

Mushroom: Suspicion

Mustard seed: Indifference

Myrrh: Gladness

Myrtle: Love in absence

Narcissus: Egotism

Nasturtium: Splendor

Nettle: Cruelty

Nightshade: Dark thoughts

Oak: Hospitality

Oleander: Beware

Olive: Peace

Orange blossom: Bridal festivities

Orange: Generosity

Palm: Victory

Pansy: Think of me

Parsley: Banquet, festivity

Pea: An appointed meeting

Peach blossom: My heart is thine

Peach: Your qualities, like your charms, are unequalled

Pear: Affection

Pennyroyal: Flee away

Peony: Shame

Peppermint: Warmth of feeling

Periwinkle: Sweet memories

Phlox: Our souls are united

Pimpernel: Rendezvous

Pine: Endurance

Pineapple: You are perfect

Pinks, double red: Pure and ardent love

Pinks, single red: Pure love

Plane tree: Genius

Plum: Keep your promises

Polyanthus: Heart's mystery

Pomegranate: Foolishness

Poplar, black: Courage

Poplar, white: Time

Poppy: Consolation

Pumpkin: Coarseness

Quince: Temptation

Ragged robin: Wit

Ranunculus: You are rich in attractions

Raspberry: Ingratitude

Reeds: Music

Reeds, split: Indiscretion

Rhododendron: Danger

Rock rose (cystus): Surety

Rose garland: Reward

Rose leaf: I never trouble

Rose, Austrian: Thou art all that is lovely

Rose, bridal: Happy love

Rose, burgundy: Unconscious beauty

Rose, cabbage: Ambassador of love

Rose, damask: Bashful love

Rose, dog (wild): Pleasure and pain

Rose, Japan: Beauty is your only attraction

Rose, moss: Voluptuous love

Rose, musk: Charming

Rose, one open and two buds: Secrecy

Rose, red and white together: Unity

Rose, tea: Always lovely

Rose, white, dried: Loss of innocence

Rose, white: I am worthy of you

Rose, yellow: Decrease of love

Rosebud, red: Confession of love

Rosebud, white: Too young to love, innocence

Rosemary: Remembrance

Rowan: I watch over you

Rudbeckia: Justice

Rue: Disdain

Rush: Docility

Saffron: Beware of excess

Sage: Esteem

Scabious: I have lost all

Scarlet lobelia: Preferment

Scotch thistle: Retaliation

Service tree: Prudence

Shamrock: Lightheartedness

Shepherd's purse: I offer thee my all

Snapdragon: Presumption

Snowdrop: Consolation

Snowdrop: Hope

Sorrel: Parental affection

Southernwood: Jesting

Speedwell: Warm feelings

Spindle tree: Thy image is engraved on my heart

St. John's wort: Animosity

Stock: Lasting beauty

Straw, broken: Quarrel

Straw, whole: Union

Strawberry: Excellence

Sunflower: False riches

Sweet pea: Departure, delicate pleasures

Sweet William: Frivolity

Sycamore: Curiosity

Tansy: I declare against thee

Tare: Vice

Thistle: Austerity

Thyme: Activity

Traveler's joy: Safety

Tuberose: Dangerous pleasures

Tulip, red: Declaration of love

Tulip, yellow: Hopeless love

Tulip, variegated: Beautiful eyes

Valerian: Accommodating disposition

Verbena: Sensibility

Veronica: Female fidelity

Vervain: Enchantment

Vine: Drunkenness

Violet, blue: Faithfulness

Violet, sweet: Modesty

Wallflower: Fidelity in adversity

Water lily: Purity of the heart

Wheat: Prosperity

Willow, common: Forsaken

Willow, weeping: Melancholy

Wolfsbane: Misanthropy

Yarrow: Cure for heartache

Yew: Sadness

Zinnia: I mourn your absence

Plant Magic

Some of the Victorian language of flowers was simply made up by its creators, while parts were based on ancient plant lore. Below is genuine magical herb craft, with some ideas on how to use the plants.

Apple

Apple blossom is associated with the summer goddess of vital energy, fertility, lust, love, and marriage, called by various names. In Welsh myth, she is the goddess Olwen, She of the White Track; in Greek, Aphrodite; and in Latin, Venus; but she has many other names around the world. The apple appears in Norse mythology in connection with love and fertility, and the goddesses Freya and Iduna.

In England, apples were often used in love divination. To discover whom she would marry, a girl would peel an apple and throw the unbroken peel over her shoulder. If it formed a letter, it was the initial of her future husband.

Apple bark, blossoms, and pips can be incorporated into incenses dedicated to the planet Venus and the element of water, or used in incense employed in the consecration of emeralds and amethysts. Apple wands are employed for love magic.

Apricot
Apricot oil is reputedly an aphrodisiac. It is used alone as a massage oil. Unfortunately it does not smell of apricots. Apricot fruits, fresh or dried, make excellent additions to the handfasting feast.

Artemisia
In the Middle East, the bitter herb artemisia is incorporated into bridal bouquets to ensure that marriages will survive bitterness as well as sweetness.

Basil
By a slight stretch of the imagination, the leaves of basil can be seen as being heart-shaped, and in folk magic this associates basil with love. In Moldavia, girls would give young men sprigs of basil as a charm to make them fall in love with them, while in Italy, girls would wear basil in the hair or rub the fragrant leaves on the skin to attract love; Spanish prostitutes still wear basil oil to attract customers. A pot of basil on a lighted windowsill was a covert invitation for a lover to call. In Voodoo, bush basil (*O. minimum*) is sacred to Erzulie, the goddess of love who is rather generous with her sexual favors. It is also sacred to Krishna, Lakshmi, and Vishnu in Hindu myth.

Basil may be employed in love incenses; the oil may be used in love and attraction oils, and the leaves in food at the handfasting feast (or seduction dinners!).

Caraway

Caraway seeds are often used at weddings, either in the cake or thrown by guests for good luck. Caraway is said to help the couple remain faithful. You might like to put some in the cake and in the ritual cup. The rings may be consecrated with caraway oil or incense.

Clove

Cloves attract the opposite sex, and increase warmth and passion. Use some cloves in the ritual cup, or warm spiced wine at the feast. Clove oil may be used in anointing and love oils. N.B. Cloves can irritate sensitive skin.

Coriander

In the Middle Ages, coriander was considered to be an aphrodisiac. The seeds were put into the popular drink *hippocras,* which was commonly drunk at Tudor weddings. Coriander is widely used in love charms and incenses, especially if the couple want their love to last beyond this lifetime, as it is a symbol of immortality. It can be included in the ritual cup for handfastings. It can also be used to anoint the candles used in love magic.

Cinnamon

In sexual or tantric magic, cinnamon oil is used to anoint the body; it stimulates the male passion with sun energy. Cinnamon sticks or powder may be mixed with other herbs in the ritual cup shared by a couple engaged in such practices, or indeed in the handfasting cup.

Clary Sage

Clary sage is a relaxing aphrodisiac. Use the essential oil in magical oils designed to attract the opposite sex, and for love and harmony, as well as for divination, prophecy, and clairvoyance. N.B. Clary sage causes drowsiness, so do not drive or operate machinery after use. Use only in small amounts and do not use at all during pregnancy.

Cumin

Cumin increases feelings of warmth and passion. Use some cumin seeds in the food or add to spiced wine.

Damiana

Damiana has a reputation as an aphrodisiac. Mexican women take damiana infusion an hour or so before the sexual act. It is believed by some to have a tonic effect on the sexual organs and the central nervous system.

The tea may be taken before Tantric practices and rites of sex magic. It may be shared by a couple performing the Great Rite. Its reputation as an aphrodisiac may come from the fact that the alkaloids have a testosterone-like action. It may be used to strengthen the male sexual system and alleviate nervous problems of a sexual origin.

Dill

Dill increases a woman's desire for a man. Use some dill seeds in the handfasting feast.

Frankincense

The ancient Egyptians used frankincense during their rituals. It is cleansing and will dissipate negative vibrations, bad atmospheres, and evil influences. It may be used before and after rituals to cleanse the atmosphere, raise vibrations, and focus the mind. It is ruled by the Sun, and is sacred to Adonis, Apollo, Bel, Demeter, Helios, Ra, and other sun gods, Venus, Vishnu, and moon goddesses.

Gardenia

Gardenia perfume increases sexual attractiveness in both men and women. It is widely used in love spells, oils, and incenses.

Ginger

Ginger is used in love spells. It increases passion, lust, and warmth. Add some to the incense, or put a pinch in the food or wine.

Hibiscus

Hibiscus attracts love and is widely used in love spells. Wear hibiscus flowers behind your ear, decorate the table with them, or use them in the bouquet and arrangements. Add some dried hibiscus petals to the incense. Drink hibiscus tea.

Ivy

The evergreen ivy is a symbol of that which is undying and eternal, the unchanging nature of the leaves making it a symbol of constancy. The Greeks used ivy to crown victors and newlyweds, and to decorate the altars of the goddess Hymen, who presided over wedding feasts and honeymoons.

Jasmine

The name jasmine derives from the Persian word *jasemin*. Persians used jasmine oil to perfume the air at banquets.

Jasmine is called "the king of flowers," and aromatherapists classify the dark essential oil, which has a faintly animal scent, as male. Conversely, in China, jasmine is associated with the feminine and female sweetness, and is symbolic of women. Hindus value the jasmine flowers very highly, and they are strung in garlands and presented to honored guests. In Borneo, it is the custom of women to roll up jasmine blossoms in their oiled hair at night to attract lovers. Jasmine is an aphrodisiac used in love sachets and incenses. Wear jasmine perfume at your pulse points for a sexual charge.

Lavender

Prostitutes wore lavender as it was believed to arouse sexual desire in men. Lavender posies were often given to newly married couples to bring luck for the future. Make some lavender ice cream for the feast.

Lemon

Use lemon in oils for love and attraction, and in sexual rituals, including the Great Rite.

Lemon Balm

Lemon balm has a happy reputation as a healing and refreshing plant. In Southern Europe, it is called "heart's delight"' and "the elixir of life." Lemon balm is connected with love shared under the influence of the Goddess. The leaves can be soaked in wine and the cup shared to strengthen the bonds between a magical group. A cup can also be shared between lovers, or employed in spells and rituals designed to attract love and money. N.B. Do not use the oil during pregnancy.

Lemon Verbena

Carrying lemon verbena is said to make you more attractive to the opposite sex.

Lotus

Hindus consider the lotus to be emblematic of the yoni. In tantra, the yoni is symbolized by a red lotus. You can use this subtle emblem in the ritual without shocking granny.

In Chinese lore, the lotus has both masculine and feminine attributes since it grows out of the yin lunar watery element into the yang, the light of the sun. It expresses spiritual unfolding with its roots in the mud, growing upward through the dark waters into the light and air. It is sacred to Kwan Yin, goddess of mercy and compassion.

The lotus is also sacred to the Canaanite goddess Quetesh, who was depicted standing on a lion holding the lotus flower in one hand and serpents in the other, and to Astarte, who is shown standing on a lion with serpents encircling her waist. She wears a crown and holds a lotus flower in each hand.

Mandarin

Mandarin oil is called the "oil of joy." It lifts the spirits and makes you glad to be alive. It is ruled by the Sun and the element of fire.

Marigold

In Tudor England, brides carried marigold (*Calendula officinalis*) dipped in rosewater and ate them afterward, since they were thought to be aphrodisiacs. The marigold means fidelity in the West. In the East, it is the flower of longevity and "the flower of ten thousand years," this being synonymous with the uncountable, the endless.

In Mexico, it was believed that marigolds (*Tagetes lucida*) grew from the spilled blood of natives killed by Spanish invaders. Marigolds were sacred to Xochiquetzal, mother of the maize god, and a goddess of flowers, sexual love, craftsmen/women, and the underworld. In her honor, marigolds were laid on graves.

Marjoram

The Greeks believed that Aphrodite created marjoram as a symbol of happiness and its scent came from her touch. Both the Greeks and the Romans used marjoram to make garlands to crown newly married couples. Marjoram was an ingredient of fourteenth-century love potions. It is associated with the Goddess of Love and may be used in handfasting garlands and incenses, or to honor or invoke love goddesses such as Venus and Aphrodite. Marjoram may be employed as a bathing herb, an incense, or a tea. Dried marjoram can also be used as an incense or tea to help clear and harmonize the heart chakra. However, aromatherapists consider that the middle note oil distilled from flowering heads of the sweet marjoram is an anaphrodisiac—it puts off potential lovers!

Meadowsweet

Also known as *bridewort, bride of the meadow,* and *mead wort,* meadowsweet falls under the dominion of Venus. It was one of the three most sacred herbs of the druids (the others were watermint and vervain). It is sometimes known as "Queen of the Meadows," which was one of the titles of the Celtic goddess Blodeuwedd ("flower-face"). Legend says that she was created from nine flowers by the sorcerers Math Mathonwy and Gwydion as a bride for the god Llew, who had been cursed by his mother Arianrhod to the effect that he should never have a mortal bride. Meadowsweet was also sacred to the Celtic goddess Aine and the "Iris Venus" Gwena.

The folk name of *bridewort* became popular because the flower was often used in bridal garlands and posies for bridesmaids. It was also frequently strewn in the church, on the path to the church, and in the home of the newlywed couples. It flowers from June through to September, and these were the most popular months for marriages in druidic times. The folk name of *mead wort* comes from the fact that it was used to flavor mead. Meadowsweet beer was an old country beverage.

Myrtle

In Greek lore, myrtle was sacred to Aphrodite, the goddess of love; at Temnos she was worshipped in the shape of a growing myrtle tree. Her attendants, the Graces, wore myrtle chaplets. The plant featured in the rites of her worship and was woven into bridal wreaths in her honor. The Romans also used it during wedding celebrations and dedicated it to the goddess of love, whom they called Venus. On April 23 they celebrated the festival of the Binalia Priora in her honor. In *Fasti*, his book on the Roman festivals, the poet Ovid wrote: "Offer her incense and pray for beauty and popular favour. Pray that you might be charming and witty. Give to the queen her own myrtle and the mint that she loves and bunches of rushes concealed in clusters of roses."

In Arabian folklore, when Adam was banished from paradise he took with him a sprig of myrtle from the bower where he first declared his love for Eve.

Northern European brides wear myrtle in honor of Freya, the love goddess. She married Odur, the summer sun. One day he went away and Freya was sad without him. Her tears fell into the sea and were transformed into amber. She set out to look for him and crossed many lands. Her tears fell and became the gold found in those places. In the sunny south, she found him beneath the flowering myrtle. They returned home, and as they passed, the flowers bloomed, the grass grew green, and the birds began to sing.

In Austria, the bride might wear a bridal wreath of myrtle over her veil, while in Britain, she gives her maids pieces of myrtle from her bouquet to bring them luck in love; if the plant roots and blossoms, they will marry soon. It was also the custom to plant a sprig from the bridal bouquet by the cottage door, and many myrtle bushes owe their existence to this. The plant was said to flourish for as long as the marriage.

Myrtle is the luckiest flower for window boxes, laying a mantle of domestic happiness over the household. Planted in the garden, it is said to ensure that love and peace reside within the home. Myrtle can be used in incenses connected with love, or in incenses dedicated to Venus or Aphrodite, Freya, and other European love goddesses.

Myrtle may be employed in handfasting rituals; it can be carried by the bride, added to the incense, or used to decorate the altar.

Neroli

Neroli is a base note oil that is distilled from the blossoms of bitter orange. It is very relaxing, and is an aphrodisiac used to attract the opposite sex.

Orange

In Greek myth, all fruit-bearing trees are the province of Demeter, goddess of marriage. In a Greek Orthodox wedding, crowns of orange blossoms were made for both bride and groom, and orange flowers were embroidered on the bride's dress.

The fragile blossoms symbolize innocence and virginity as well as fidelity, eternal love, and fertility. Saracenic brides carried sprigs of orange blossom, and the tradition was introduced into Europe during the Crusades, though not in Britain, as the climate is too cold to support orange trees, except in the very expensive glassed "orangeries" that were once enjoyed by the aristocracy. The orange tree has a magical reputation because it produces buds, flowers, and fruit at the same time.

Patchouli

Patchouli oil is a base note perfume that is distilled from the dried leaves of the patchouli plant. It has an aphrodisiac effect, stimulating sensuality and sexuality, and is therefore used in love and attraction oils. The oil is also useful as a fixative in perfumes and incense. Small quantities are uplifting, whereas larger doses have a sedative effect.

Rose

The generic name *rosa* comes from the Greek *rodon,* meaning "red," as the roses of the ancients were a deep crimson color. Aphrodite, the goddess of love, first emerged from the sea at the island of Cyprus, and where she stepped to shore, the sea foam fell to earth in the form of white roses. In one tale, red roses were created when she scratched herself on a white rose while pursuing her lover Adonis, and it became colored by her blood. In another, it was Adonis' shed blood that caused red roses to bloom. The white rose represents purity and innocence, while the red rose stands for passion.

The rose has always been an emblem of love, sacred to all goddesses of love. They were considered to be an aphrodisiac. It is said that Cleopatra seduced Anthony while standing knee-deep in roses. In Britain, rose petals were scattered at weddings to ensure a happy marriage. In alchemy, the rose symbolizes mystical or divine love. Red and white roses together signify the union of opposites, the blending of fire and water; red signifies the masculine, the king, and white is feminine, the queen. This symbolism is echoed in the Tudor rose, a symbol of reconciliation employed after the ending of the Wars of the Roses (1485) when the white rose of the House of York and the red rose of Lancaster were joined.

The Romans used the rose garlands at feasts, and guests were sometimes showered with rose petals, though at one banquet, so many petals cascaded down that some of the company were suffocated! Roman brides and bridegrooms were crowned with roses, as were images of Cupid, Venus, and Bacchus. Roses were scattered at the feasts of Flora and Hymen, in the paths of victors, and on the prows of war vessels. May 23 was the Roman rose festival the *Rosalia,* in honor of the goddess Flora.

The rose symbolizes love and the sacred marriage of the God and Goddess. Rose petals can be added to the cup into which the athame is plunged in obvious symbolism. The invoking priestess might wear a chaplet of roses. Petals can be scattered around the circle in an act of blessing. Roses speak to us of the divine love of the Lord and Lady, the fruits of which bring life to the earth.

Rose oil is a useful oil for women, treating impurities in the womb, irregular periods, and depression. It is ruled by the planet Venus and the element of water, and is used for spells of love, attraction, marriage, and sensuality. It brings about a calm, peaceful atmosphere and induces harmony.

Rosemary

The Greek and Romans believed that rosemary symbolized both love and death. Traces of rosemary have been found in ancient Egyptian tombs. In some places rosemary is a wedding herb, and all guests are given a branch of rosemary wrapped in gold and ribbons as a keepsake, so that they might remember the day. Occasionally, rosemary was used as a garland for brides, even for queens. In the past, the wood was utilized in the manufacture of the musical instruments that accompanied love songs. In the Victorian language of flowers, rosemary is seen as the symbol of fidelity, love, remembrance, and friendship. Sprinkle powdered rosemary under the marriage bed to keep a couple together.

Sandalwood

Sandalwood oil is a base note perfume that is steam distilled from the small drips and raspings of the heartwood of the tree. It has aphrodisiac properties and is used in love and attraction oils, and those used during sex rituals, including the Great Rite. Sandalwood chips may be added to the handfasting incense.

Vervain

Some people believe that the name of this herb was derived from *Herba veneris,* a name given to the plant by the Romans because of its aphrodisiac qualities. The Romans held that vervain was sacred to Venus, the goddess of love, while to the Greeks it was sacred to Aphrodite, the root being worn by her priests in their robes. The ancient Egyptians believed that vervain had been formed from the tears of Isis. For centuries, vervain retained its reputation as an herb of love and was a prime ingredient of love potions. Vervain was one of the three most sacred herbs of the druids.

Violet

The Greeks saw the violet as a symbol of fertility, sacred to Aphrodite, who is attended by the Three Graces, who weave her robes and plait her crown of violets. When she steps onto the shore, violet flowers and roses spring up beneath her feet. The Romans also believed the violet to be a symbol of love, and both they and the Greeks drank violet wine. Violets are seen as a symbol of the constancy of love and fertility. Because of this, they were often carried in love sachets, sometimes mixed with lavender to attract a new love, and frequently added to love potions. Violets are also sacred to the Goddess of Love and may be used in incenses, garlands, and temple decorations to invoke and honor her.

Yarrow

One of yarrow's folk names, *seven year's love,* refers to the fact that it was thought to have the property of being able to keep couples loving and faithful for seven years if incorporated into the wedding bouquet.

Ylang Ylang

A base note oil, ylang ylang is a calming, relaxing oil that lifts the spirits and engenders feelings of peace and harmony. It can be used for sexual problems, as it has aphrodisiac qualities. Use ylang ylang in oils of love and attraction. It is ruled by Venus and the element of water.

The Bridal Wreath

The bridal wreath or chaplet of flowers is another circular symbol of eternity and perfection, reinforcing the idea of love as part of the cycle of life. Choose your favorite flowers and flower symbolism. The wreath can be easily constructed using the following items:

Thick florist's wire

Thin florist's wire

Green florist's tape

Flowers

Ribbons

Use the thick wire to make a circle fitting the bride's head. Leave a little extra space to accommodate the flowers and tape. Bind the flowers to the circle using the thinner wires and cover with the green tape.

Bind the flowers close together and intersperse with greenery and gypsophillia for a really stunning look. Add colored ribbons at the back.

Alternatively, you might purchase a bridal crown or tiara and cover this with flowers or herbs.

The Bouquet

It is possible that the Stone Age bride went to her nuptials carrying a posy of wild flowers, though it is unlikely that we will ever know for sure when the custom first began. Certainly it is ancient and very widespread. In ancient Rome, Greece, and Egypt, brides carried sheaths of wheat and grains. This developed into a loose bunch of flowers, and during the Middle Ages, English brides carried posies or nosegays of sweet-smelling flowers and herbs.

I feel it is much lovelier to make your own bouquet, preferably with wild flowers or flowers from your garden, or to have it made by a friend as an act of love rather than just buying one from a professional florist. In the past, the bouquet was usually made for the bride by her mother.

Different flowers have always been considered as having certain virtues and a magical significance, and this has already been discussed earlier in this chapter. An old English custom is to have love knots of ribbon hanging from the bouquet.

Incenses

Loose incense is probably the easiest type of incense to make, and the most useful kind for magical ritual. The recipes in this book are all for loose incense.

First of all, assemble your ingredients, your pestle and mortar, your mixing spoons and your jars and labels ready for the finished product. All the measurements in this book are by volume, not weight. I use a spoon to measure out small quantities when I am making a single jar of incense, or a cup for large quantities and big batches. Therefore when the recipe says 3 parts frankincense, 1/2 part thyme, and 1 part myrrh, this means three spoonfuls of frankincense, half a spoonful of thyme, and one spoonful of myrrh.

When using resins and essential oils, these should be combined together first, stirring lightly with the pestle and left to go a little sticky before you add any woods, barks, and crushed berries. Next add any herbs and powders and lastly any flowers.

As you blend the incense, concentrate on the purpose for which the incense will be used, and "project" this into the blend. If you'd like, you can make a whole ritual of the event, perhaps even picking and drying your own herbs, then laying out the tools and ingredients on the altar, lighting a candle, and asking the God and Goddess for help:

> *God and Goddess, deign to bless this incense which I would conse-crate in your names. Let it obtain the necessary virtues for acts of love and beauty in your honor. Let Blessing Be.*

The incenses should then be stored in screw-topped glass jars.

Burning Incenses

Loose incense is burned on individual self-igniting charcoal blocks, or thrown directly onto the bonfire.

To use your incenses, take a self-igniting charcoal block (available from occult and church suppliers) and apply a match to it. It will begin to spark across its surface, and eventually will glow red. Place it on a flameproof dish with a mat underneath (it will get very hot). When the charcoal block is glowing, sprinkle a pinch of the incense on top—a little goes a long way. Alternatively, if you are celebrating outdoors and have a bonfire, you can throw much larger quantities of incense directly onto the flames.

A useful tip is when a packet of charcoal blocks has been opened, they will quickly start to absorb moisture from the air, which makes them difficult to ignite. Pop them in the oven for ten minutes on a low heat to dry them out, and they will light easily.

The method for each of the following recipes is the same: Mix the ingredients together and burn on charcoal.

Handfasting Incense

3 parts frankincense

1 part copal

1 part red rose petals

A few drops rose oil

A few drops orange oil

½ part cinnamon powder

Love Incense

½ part thyme

3 parts red sandalwood

1 part red rose petals

A few drops lavender oil

½ part lavender flowers

½ part basil leaves

Love Incense #2

½ part thyme

3 parts red sandalwood

1 part red rose petals

A few drops bergamot oil

A few drops lavender oil

½ part lavender flowers

½ part basil

True Love Incense

3 parts frankincense

A few drops patchouli oil

½ part orris root

½ part cinnamon root

Eros Incense (Greek god of love)

1 part red rose petals

½ part bay leaves

1 part dog rose petals

4 parts acacia resin

Freya Incense (Teutonic moon/love goddess)

½ part primrose flowers

½ part cowslip flowers

½ part cypress needles

1 part mistletoe twigs and leaves

½ part rose petals

½ part daisy petals

½ part strawberry leaves

½ part myrtle

½ part red clover flowers

5 parts myrrh

2 parts benzoin

3 parts red sandalwood

A few drops rose oil (optional)

A few drops sandalwood oil

Hulda Incense (Teutonic goddess of marriage and fertility)

1 part flax flowers

1 part rose petals

1 part dog rose hips

2 parts elder wood

½ part elder blossoms

Aphrodite Incense (Greek goddess of love)

½ part cypress needles

A few drops cypress oil

3 parts benzoin

½ part rose petals

1 part apple wood

¼ part cinnamon sticks

¼ part daisy flowers

A few drops geranium oil

¼ part violet flowers

Astarte Incense (Canaanite fertility goddess)

3 parts acacia

1 part myrtle blossoms

1 part pine wood

½ part pine resin

A few drops pine oil

2 parts sandalwood

1 part red rose petals

A few drops orange oil

1 part jasmine flowers

3 parts frankincense

Apollo Incense
(Greek and Roman god of the sun, poetry, and medicine)

½ part bay laurel leaves

½ part peony flowers

2 parts aspen wood

2 parts frankincense

½ part cypress needles

½ part fennel seeds

2 parts acacia

A few drops bay oil

Adonis Incense (Greek vegetation god)

½ part fir needles

1 part myrrh

½ part anemone flowers

2 parts frankincense

1 part acacia resin
A few drops bay oil
½ part narcissus flowers

Bride Incense
1 part heather flowers
3 parts myrrh
½ part celandine
½ part angelica flowers
½ part basil

Cernunnos Incense (Celtic horned god)
½ part betony herb
1 part pine resin
A few drops pine oil
2 parts oak wood
½ part camomile flowers
½ part yarrow herb
1 part lavender flowers
1 part cedar wood
1 part ash wood
½ part bistort root
½ part nettle herb

Cupid Incense (Roman god of love)
1 part rose petals
A few drops rose oil
1 part cypress needles
½ part bay leaves
½ part dog rose hips

Demeter Incense (Greek corn goddess)
½ part grains of corn
1 part rose petals

2 parts frankincense

2 parts myrrh

½ part pennyroyal herb

½ part bean flowers

½ part red poppy petals

½ part cypress needles

A few drops rose oil (optional)

A few drops cypress oil

Eros Incense (Greek god of love)

1 part red rose petals

½ part bay leaves

½ part dog rose hips

A few drops rose oil

1 part frankincense

1 part myrrh

Erzulie Incense (Haitian Voodoo goddess of love)

1 part basil herb

2 parts crushed cardamom pods

Hera Incense (Greek Queen of Heaven)

1 part apple blossom

2 parts willow

½ part iris petals

A few drops cypress oil

½ part red poppy petals

3 parts myrrh

1 part pear bark

Juno Incense (Roman Queen of Heaven)

3 parts myrrh

A few drops myrrh oil

½ part olive leaves

½ part iris petals

½ part orris root powder

Magical Oils

Magical oils can be used in several ways:

- In the bath—Add two teaspoons of blended magical oil to the bath after it has run. Swirl it about in the water to ensure dispersion over the surface. As you get into the bath, the oil will coat your skin, and the heat of the water helps its absorption. You will also breathe in the vapors. For an oil bath, do not use soap—treat it as a ritual, not a wash. A purification bath is a prerequisite to any ritual, and you can add an appropriate oil to help you attune to the ceremony to come.

- Anointing—Most magical groups anoint coveners as they enter the circle, during initiation handfasting rituals, etc. Magical tools are anointed as part of their consecration.

- Vaporization—All essential oils readily evaporate and may be used in the place of incense if this is more convenient. Bear in mind that in this case they represent the element of fire rather than air, within the circle. Purpose-made oil evaporators should be used.

- An oil may be used to "seal" a doorway or window against negativity after a cleansing or exorcism has taken place. A suitable oil is smeared around the opening.

- Do not take any of the oils internally. The oils are highly concentrated and can be damaging or even poisonous when taken internally.

Types of Oils

There are two types of magical oils that I use. The first type I make from herbs and flowers that I collect or grow. It is impossible to make essential oils at home, so I make infused oils (see the next section).

The second type I make are blended oils, made with a base oil and drops of store-bought pure essential oils added.

Making Infused Oils

Loosely fill a clear glass jar with freshly picked sprigs of herbs or flowers. Fill the jar with a vegetable oil (almond and sunflower are best). Cover the top of the jar with a piece of muslin and leave on a sunny windowsill for about two weeks, stirring daily. Strain into a clean jar or bottle. This oil will keep for around four to five months in a cool, dark place. There is no need to dilute it any further for use, but you can blend together several varieties if you wish.

Making Blended Oils

The recipes in this book are for blended oils. They are formulated using 20 ml of base oil (see the next section) and the stated number of drops of essential oil. Essential oils are readily available. They are quite expensive, but a little goes a long way—you only use a few drops at a time. Try buying three or four 5 ml bottles to begin with, and then gradually build up your collection. Undiluted essential oils stored in a cool, dark environment will last for several years. Essential oils are far too concentrated to use alone. They could cause serious damage if used undiluted. Always make sure that you buy *100% pure essential oils* from a reputable supplier. Perfume oils are synthetic and have no therapeutic or magical effect. If you wish the oil to keep for longer than a few weeks, you will have to use a base of wheatgerm oil, or add 20–30 drops of pure vitamin E oil to the blend. I have oils that have kept for years based on this prescription.

Base Oils

Base oils, which make up the bulk of your formula, should be vegetable in origin—never use mineral oils, including baby oil. Suitable oils include avocado, hazelnut, wheatgerm, grapeseed, olive, sunflower, rapeseed, soya, and almond. You will find most of them in the supermarket (yes, the same stuff you cook with!).

Lord and Lady Oil

10 drops rose, 4 drops cinnamon, 3 drops myrrh, 3 drops frankincense

Love Oil

5 drops bergamot, 5 drops lavender, 1 drop clove, 1 drop cinnamon

Love Drawing Oil

15 drops rose, 5 drops lavender

Anointing Oil

4 drops myrrh, 4 drops cinnamon

Cleopatra's Seduction Oil

5 drops jasmine, 5 drops myrrh, 3 drops frankincense, 8 drops rose

Consecration Oil

4 drops clove, 8 drops lemongrass, 8 drops thyme

Temple Oil

3 drops rosemary, 3 drops frankincense, 4 drops thyme

Goddess Venus Love Oil

2 drops verbena, 5 drops lemon, 5 drops orange

Venus Planetary Oil

7 drops thyme, 9 drops cedar, 4 drops benzoin

Making Magical Bath Salts

Take 1 ounce or 28 grams of salt and place in a nonporous ceramic basin. Add a total of 6–8 drops of undiluted essential oil (see the previous section on magical oil recipes and adapt these to the required amount). Blend in with a pestle and place in an airtight jar. If you'd like, you can add color in the form of food coloring as a further resonance of magic. This color should be added before the oil and blended until it is smooth throughout. The bath salts may be used in the pre-ritual bath for cleansing the body and aura, and to help you attune to the matter at hand.

Chapter 10

THE HANDFASTING
FEAST

*A*round the world there are many different traditional wedding foods. Here in Britain, the wedding cake is a rich, iced cake, full of nuts and fruit that represent fertility and prosperity, since such ingredients were once very rare and expensive. The Icelandic wedding cake is called *kransakaka* and consists of rings of almond pastry of various sizes piled on top of one another, decorated with swirls of icing, while the hollow center is filled with sweets and chocolate. The Dutch feast is characterized by a sweet called "bridal sugar" and spiced wine called "bride's tears." In the Mediterranean, breads take center stage, and are often decorated with beads and flowers. The bride and groom are offered a cake made of honey, sesame seed, and quince. Italian wedding banquets may include as many as fourteen courses, ending with a range of desserts such as sugar-coated almonds, twists of fried sugared dough, heart-shaped biscuits, and so on.

Greek weddings feature nuts, with sugar-coated almonds, or *koufetta*, placed in odd numbers in little bags; the odd number signifies that they are undividable, and the couple must share them. The koufetta are also carried to guests on a silver tray; if an unmarried woman takes them off the tray and puts them under her pillow, she will dream of the man she'll marry. On some of the Greek islands, the wedding ceremony ends with honey and walnuts offered to the bride and groom from silver spoons. Walnuts easily break into four parts, standing for the bride, groom, and their two families.

Chinese weddings are a demonstration of the generosity and wealth of the family, featuring elaborate twelve-course banquets with enough left over to feed the poor. Things are simpler in Korea, where a simple "noodle feast" is served, consisting of a single dish of long noodles, which symbolize a long and happy life.

The hot spices, such as ginger, cinnamon, cumin, cardamom, anise, and clove, are said to promote sexual energy and passion. Anise was an ingredient of the Roman wedding cake, the forerunner of our own traditional iced fruit cake. Caraway is said to help lovers remain faithful, while dill strengthens the bonds of a couple. Coriander is an herb of love and harmony and has been used in love charms for hundreds, if not thousands, of years. Cinnamon and yarrow stimulate male sexual energy.

Some ingredients honor the Goddess of Love and her gifts, such as meadowsweet, strawberry, saffron, apple, sorrel, mallow, violet, peppermint, catmint, and red roses. Clove, basil, apricot, lemon, lime, vanilla, and lemon balm attract love. Both rosemary and violet mark boundaries and rites of passage—the passage from the single state to the married one, the leaving behind of one life and the beginning of a new one as a couple. Marjoram helps harmonize the heart chakra and promotes unselfish love.

The period after the marriage is called "the honeymoon" from the practice of the ancient Germans of drinking honey wine for thirty days after the marriage. Honey was widely believed to be an aphrodisiac in ancient and medieval times and was an indispensable ingredient of love potions and spells, or was taken with food and wine.

Savory Dishes

Cheese and Hazelnut Paté

4 ounces Lancashire cheese (or fontina cheese, if Lancashire cheese is
  not available)

4 ounces hazelnuts (½ cup)

4 ounces butter (½ cup or 1 stick butter)

Method

Blend all the ingredients together in a food processor, or grind with a
pestle and mortar until smooth.

Hazelnut Tart

8 ounces whole wheat pastry shell (for a single crust pie)

1 onion

1 ounce butter or margarine (2 tablespoons)

3 ounces ground hazelnuts (6 tablespoons)

2 eggs, beaten

¼ pint vegetable stock (½ cup)

1 teaspoon Marmite or Vegemite (yeast extract—available in many
  health food or gourmet stores)

1 tablespoon fresh sage, chopped

Salt and pepper

Method

Line a flan dish with the pastry. Cook the finely chopped onion in the
butter over medium heat and add the other ingredients. Pour into the
pastry shell and bake in a moderate oven at 350°F/180°C/gas mark 4
for 40 minutes.

Nut Roast

1 onion

1 tablespoon oil

1 ounce flour (2 tablespoons)

¼ pint vegetable stock (½ cup)

Mixed herbs to taste

½ teaspoon Marmite or Vegemite (yeast extract—available in many
    health food or gourmet food stores)

12 ounces ground mixed nuts (1½ cups)

4 ounces brown breadcrumbs (½ cup)

1 ounce rolled oats (2 tablespoons)

4 tomatoes

4 ounces mushrooms (½ cup sliced)

2 eggs, beaten

Salt and pepper to taste

Method

Heat a medium skillet and add the oil. Chop the onion and cook over
medium heat in the oil until soft. Add the flour and vegetable stock
and stir to thicken. Add the herbs and Marmite, and simmer over low
heat for five minutes. Remove from heat. Meanwhile, in a large bowl,
mix the nuts, breadcrumbs, oats, tomatoes, mushrooms, and season-
ing. Add the beaten eggs and the cooled onion gravy. Mix thoroughly.
Spoon into a greased 2-pound loaf pan and bake for 30-40 minutes at
375°F/190°C/gas mark 5.

Coll Cakes

6 ounces ground hazelnuts (¾ cup)

½ cup honey

1 ounce flour (2 tablespoons)

1 tablespoon grated lemon peel

1 egg, beaten

1 tablespoon lemon juice

Method

Blend the honey and nuts into a paste. Mix in the flour and lemon
peel. Blend the egg and lemon juice together and add to the mixture.
Drop small amounts onto a greased baking tray and bake at 350°F/
180°C/gas mark 4 for 20 minutes.

Basil and Love-Apple Mold

1 pound tomatoes
2 cloves garlic, crushed
Handful of basil, shredded
1 teaspoon sugar
½ pint tomato purée (1 cup)
Tabasco sauce
Worcestershire sauce
Juice of half a lemon
Stale bread slices
Salt and pepper to taste
Olive oil

Method

Scald and peel tomatoes. Chop roughly. Stir garlic, basil, and sugar into tomatoes and season with salt and pepper. Put the tomato purée in a shallow dish and stir in a dash of Tabasco sauce, a dash of Worcestershire sauce, and the lemon juice. Cut one slice of bread to fit the base of a 1-quart casserole dish and dip it into the purée mixture, coating both sides. Place the coated bread in the bottom of the dish. Cut the other slices to fit around the inside of the dish, coating them in the purée mixture before pressing into place. Pour in the tomatoes, basil, and garlic. Drizzle olive oil over the surface and top with more coated bread. Place a weighted plate on the top and put in the refrigerator overnight, remembering to put a plate underneath to catch any spillage. Turn out onto a plate and serve with salad.

Herb Salad

½ pound tomatoes, seeded and sliced (¾ cup)
½ cucumber, seeded and sliced
1 sweet red pepper, seeded and sliced
6 scallions, chopped
½ head of lettuce, shredded
1 small sprig thyme, finely chopped

Dressing:
1 sprig marjoram, finely chopped
2 tarragon leaves, finely chopped
¼ pint plain yogurt (½ cup)

Method
Mix together the herbs and the yogurt. Arrange all the other ingredients in a salad dish and dress with the yogurt mixture.

Sweet Dishes

Handfasting Cake
3 ounces butter (6 tablespoons)
4 ounces superfine sugar (½ cup)
½ pint milk (1 cup)
2 egg whites
Pinch of salt
1 teaspoon baking powder
5 ounces plain flour (⅔ cup)
2 ounces candied lemon or orange peel (¼ cup)
1 heaping teaspoon caraway seeds

Method
Grease an 8-inch round cake pan. Cut a piece of parchment paper the size of the bottom of the pan. Place paper in pan and grease lightly. Cream together the butter and sugar and stir in the milk. Whip the egg whites until stiff and gently fold into the butter mixture. Add the salt, baking powder, and flour. Add the candied peel and caraway seeds. Pour into the prepared baking pan and bake in a moderate oven at 350°F/180°C/gas mark 4 for 60 minutes or until brown and a skewer or cake tester inserted in the cake comes out clean.

Lemon and Ginger Muffins
1 pound white unbleached flour (3½ cups)
1 level teaspoon salt

¼ pint cold milk (½ cup)
¼ pint boiling water (½ cup)
1 package dry yeast
1 egg, beaten
1 ounce melted butter (2 tablespoons)
Finely grated rind of 1 lemon
1 teaspoon dry ginger

Method

Sift together the flour and salt. In a jug, mix together the milk and water, and stir a little into the yeast to make a cream. Pour this cream into the milk and water and stir well. Mix into the flour with the egg to form a soft dough, and then add the melted butter. Turn out onto a floured board and knead until it is no longer sticky (adding more flour as needed). Cover and leave in a warm place until it has doubled in size. Knead again on a floured board sprinkled with the lemon rind and ginger, so that they are incorporated into the dough. Roll out to ½-inch thick. Cut into rounds with a 3-inch cutter and arrange them on a well-floured baking tray, allowing space between each. Dust the rounds with flour. Cover again and leave them to double in size. Bake at the top of the oven at 450°F/250°C/gas mark 8 for 5 minutes.

Ginger Roll

1 200-gram or 8-ounce package gingersnaps
½ pint whipping cream (1 cup)
1 glass dry sherry (2 fluid ounces or ¼ cup)
Fruit leftover from a fresh fruit salad

Method

Whip the cream until very stiff. Pour the sherry into a small bowl and dip a gingersnap into the sherry. Spread the softened gingersnap with whipped cream. Do the same with a second gingersnap and sandwich them together, plain side to creamed, and stand them on edge to form the beginning of the log. If desired, you can place a small piece of fruit in between each gingersnap. Continue in this way with the remaining gingersnaps, until your log is of the desired length (2–3 inches). Cover with the rest of the cream and chill thoroughly for at least half an hour. Decorate with more fruit and serve. The gingersnaps will have softened and will melt deliciously in the mouth.

Tudor Flan

3 tablespoons honey
¼ pint water (½ cup)
2 oranges, thinly sliced
1 pie shell (for a single crust pie)
¼ pint heavy cream, whipped (½ cup)
2 ounces sugar (¼ cup)

Method

Mix the honey and water in a medium bowl. Drop in the orange slices and let stand overnight. The next day, place the orange mixture in a pan. Bring to a boil, reduce heat, and simmer for 30 minutes. Line a flan dish with the pastry and bake undisturbed in a hot oven at 425°F/220°C/gas mark 7 for 15 minutes. Remove from oven and let cool on a wire rack. Meanwhile, drain the oranges from the syrup and leave to cool slightly. Spread the bottom of the pastry shell with the cream and arrange the orange slices on top. Add the sugar to the syrup, and bring to a boil. Reduce heat and simmer for 5 minutes until the liquid thickens. Spoon over the orange slices.

Honeydew Cake

2 teaspoons lemon juice
Pinch of saffron
6 ounces white unbleached flour (¾ cup)
½ teaspoon baking soda
1 teaspoon cinnamon
¼ teaspoon ground cloves
⅓ cup butter

3 ounces light brown sugar (6 tablespoons)
3 tablespoons honey
2 tablespoons corn syrup (golden syrup)
1 egg, beaten

To decorate:
1 ounce softened butter (2 tablespoons)
3 ounces powdered sugar (6 tablespoons)
2 tablespoons honey

Method
Set the oven at 350°F/180°C/gas mark 4. Put the saffron to soak in the lemon juice. Lightly grease a 7-inch cake pan, preferably a heart-shaped one, and line the base with parchment paper. Lightly grease the paper. Sift the flour, soda, cinnamon, and cloves into a bowl and make a well in the center. Put the butter and sugar into a pan with the honey and syrup and melt over a low heat. Pour this mixture into the flour well, and mix with a wooden spoon. Add the beaten egg and saffron/lemon juice, and continue beating until smooth. Pour into the pan and bake in the center of the oven for 35–40 minutes. Cool on a wire rack for 5 minutes and then invert out onto the rack. Remove the paper. To decorate, beat together the butter, powdered sugar, and honey. Spread over the top of the cake and place in the refrigerator to set. This cake is best made a few days in advance as the flavor improves with refrigeration. Wrapped, it will keep for around 14 days. The top can be decorated with crystallized ginger, crystallized violets, strawberries, or any seasonal, edible flowers or fruit.

Bridal Cake
8 ounces butter, softened (1 cup)
8 ounces sugar (1 cup)
3 tablespoons honey
Zest of 1 orange, grated
4 eggs
2 tablespoons liqueur (Cointreau, peach brandy, or whatever you like)

12 ounces white unbleached flour (1½ cups)
1 teaspoon baking powder
Pinch of salt
2 ounces ground almonds
1 pound 4 ounces chopped dried fruit (2½ cups)
4 ounces chopped candied cherries (½ cup) (glacé cherries)

For the topping:
Halved nuts
Crystallized fruit
Apricot jam

Method
Set the oven at 350°F/180°C/gas mark 4. Cream the butter and sugar. Beat in the honey and orange rind and add the beaten eggs a little at a time. If the mixture curdles, add a little flour. Add the liqueur. Fold in the flour, baking powder, and salt, and then the mixed fruit, almonds, and cherries. Grease an 8-inch cake pan, and line with greased parchment paper. Spoon batter into prepared pan and bake in the center of the oven for 45 minutes. Reduce the temperature to 325°F/170°C/gas mark 3 and continue to cook for about 1½ hours. Remove from the oven and cool in the pan for ½ hour. The cake may be wrapped in paper and foil and stored in a pan until ready for use. To decorate, remove all the wrappings. Glaze with apricot jam and arrange the fruit and nuts on top.

Rosemary Fruit Cake
6 ounces butter, softened (¾ cup)
6 ounces soft brown sugar (¾ cup)
3 eggs, beaten
8 ounces white unbleached flour (1 cup)
1 teaspoon baking powder
1 pound mixed dried fruit, chopped (4 cups)
1 tablespoon chopped fresh rosemary leaves

Method

Grease an 8-inch cake pan and line with greased parchment paper. Cream the butter and sugar and gradually beat in the eggs. Fold in the flour and the baking powder. Add the fruit and rosemary. Spoon into the pan. Cook at 325°F/170°C/gas mark 3 for about 1½ hours. Reduce the temperature to 300°F/150°C/gas mark 2 and cook for another hour. Cool in the pan. When ready to serve, invert onto a plate and remove the parchment paper.

Ginger Cake

4 ounces butter, softened (½ cup)
4 ounces brown sugar (½ cup)
2 ounces molasses (¼ cup) (black treacle)
2 ounces corn syrup (¼ cup) (golden syrup)
1 egg
8 ounces white unbleached flour (1 cup)
1 teaspoon ground ginger
½ teaspoon baking soda
2 tablespoons milk

Method

Cream the butter and sugar. Warm the molasses and corn syrup and add to the butter and sugar. Gradually add the beaten egg, flour, and ginger. Dissolve the baking soda in the milk and add to the mixture. Grease an 8-inch cake pan and spoon in the cake mix. Bake at 300°F/150°C/gas mark 2 for 1 hour.

Irish Whiskey Cake

2¼ pounds mixed dried sultanas, raisins, and currants (4½ cups)
2 ounces mixed lemon and orange peel (¼ cup)
2 ounces candied cherries (¼ cup) (glacé cherries)
2 ounces chopped walnuts (¼ cup)
¼ pint whiskey (½ cup)
¼ pint milk (½ cup)
12 ounces dark brown sugar (1½ cups)

12 ounces butter, softened (1½ cups)

4 eggs, beaten

1 pound 4 ounces white unbleached flour (2½ cups)

1 tablespoon baking powder

2 level teaspoons Pumpkin Pie spice (or an equivalent mixture of cinnamon, ginger, allspice, and nutmeg—also called missed spice)

To glaze:

2 tablespoons apricot jam

Method

Place the dried fruit and peel in a bowl. Stir in the whiskey and milk. Cover and leave overnight. Heat the oven to 275°F/140°C/gas mark 1. Oil a large baking pan (approximately 12 x 10 x 2 inches) and line the base and sides with parchment paper. Brush the paper with oil. Cream the butter and sugar, and add the beaten eggs a little at a time. If the mixture curdles, add a little flour. Sift the flour, baking powder, and spices and fold into the creamed mixture. Add the fruit, nuts, and whiskey. Stir well. Turn into the prepared baking pan. Bake in the center of the oven for 2¼–2½ hours. Cool in the pan. Invert onto a serving plate and remove the paper. If you really must, you can sprinkle more whiskey over the cake and brush the top with warmed strained apricot jam. Cut into portions and wrap in waxed paper or foil until ready to eat.

English Wedding Cake

9 ounces white unbleached flour (1⅛ cup)

1 teaspoon Pumpkin Pie spice (or an equivalent mixture of cinnamon, ginger, allspice, and nutmeg—also called missed spice)

½ teaspoon ground cinnamon

8 ounces butter, softened (1 cup)

8 ounces light brown sugar (1 cup)

4 eggs, beaten

1½ tablespoons molasses (black treacle)

¼ cup lemon or orange peel

2½ pounds mixed fruit (5 cups)
2 ounces chopped blanched almonds (¼ cup)
3 ounces candied cherries (6 tablespoons) (glacé cherries)
3 tablespoons rum

Method

Sift together flour, mixed spice, and cinnamon in a large bowl. In a separate bowl, cream together the butter and sugar until very pale and fluffy. Beat in the eggs a little at a time, adding a little of the flour mixture to prevent the eggs from curdling. Stir in the molasses and the flour mixture, together with the mixed fruit, peel, cherries, and nuts. Stir until well combined. Double-line the bottom and sides of an 8-inch cake pan with greased parchment paper. To insulate the pan and prevent the cake from burning, tie a band of doubled brown paper around the outside, so that it comes 1 inch above the side of the pan. Pour the cake mixture into the pan and bake in a cool oven at 300°F/150°C/gas mark 2 for 3 hours. Reduce the heat to 275°F/140°C/gas mark 1 and continue cooking for another 50 minutes or until a skewer inserted comes out clean. Leave the cake in the pan for 10 minutes, during which time it will shrink away from the sides. Turn onto a wire cooling rack. When cool, but not cold, turn the cake upside down and make holes in the bottom with a skewer. Spoon the rum over and allow it to soak in. Leave until cold and then wrap and store in an airtight container. When ready to serve, drizzle the cake with a little more rum, over the top this time, and then coat with marzipan and icing as desired, perhaps with silver decorations. *The cake should be made six weeks to a month before the event and iced one week before.*

Amorette

½ pound strawberries, washed and hulled (1 cup)
¾ pint light cream (1½ cups)
¼ pint milk (½ cup)
2 ounces sugar (¼ cup)
3 egg yolks

Method

Purée strawberries. Place the cream, milk, and sugar in a pan and bring almost to a boil. Stir in the strawberry purée. Reheat again to near boiling point. Remove from heat. Beat the eggs in a clean bowl. Beat in some of the hot cream mixture, and then add back to the cream in the pan. Heat gently until the mixture is thick enough to coat the back of a spoon. Cool. Place in the freezer. When it is half frozen, whisk thoroughly and return it to the freezer. After 1 hour, whisk again, and do the same after another hour.

Inamorata

6 ounces dark chocolate, broken

4 eggs, separated

1 pint heavy cream (2 cups)

2 handfuls of fresh peppermint leaves, chopped

4 ounces superfine sugar (½ cup)

Method

Melt 4 ounces of the chocolate in a double boiler, over boiling water. Remove from the heat and gradually whisk in the egg yolks. Leave to cool. Meanwhile, whip the cream until stiff. Add the chopped peppermint leaves and gradually fold into the chocolate mixture. Put in the freezer until the ice cream begins to set at the edges and then whisk again. Return to the freezer for 45 minutes, then whisk once more. Repeat this procedure until the ice cream is set. Whisk the egg whites until stiff but not dry, and fold in the superfine sugar. Carefully fold this into the frozen ice cream. Return to the freezer until the ice cream is completely set. Serve with mint leaves dipped in melted chocolate.

Cara Sposa

1 pound strawberries, washed and hulled (2 cups)

½ pint water (1 cup)

3 ounces sugar (6 tablespoons)

1 egg white

Method

Purée the strawberries. In a pan, bring the water and sugar to a boil and stir until the sugar dissolves. Allow to cool. Stir in the puréed strawberries and pour into ice cube trays. Freeze for 30 minutes. Meanwhile, whisk the egg white until it forms stiff peaks. Remove the fruit mixture from the freezer and turn out into a bowl. Beat until creamy. Fold in the egg white. Put back in the trays and freeze until set—at least 1 hour.

Tryst

½ pint water (1 cup)

Generous handful of scented geranium (*Pelargonium graveolens*) leaves

3 ounces sugar (6 tablespoons)

1 egg white

A few drops pure lemon oil or lemon flavoring

A few mint leaves to garnish

Method

In a pan, bring the water, geranium leaves, and sugar to a boil and stir until the sugar dissolves. Remove from heat and steep for 1 hour. Remove the leaves, squeezing them to obtain as much flavor as possible, and pour the liquid into ice cube trays. Freeze for 30 minutes. Meanwhile, whisk the egg white until it forms stiff peaks. Remove the mixture from the freezer and turn into a bowl. Add the lemon oil and beat until creamy. Fold in the egg white. Put back in the trays and freeze until set—at least 1 hour.

Sweethearts

1 pound powdered sugar (2 cups) (plus additional powdered sugar
  for the countertop)

¼ pound cornstarch (½ cup) (cornflour)

½–1 teaspoon strawberry extract or flavoring

Evaporated milk

Chocolate to coat

Method

Sift together the cornstarch and sugar. Stir in the strawberry extract. Thoroughly mix in enough evaporated milk to form a stiff but workable paste, and knead until well combined. Turn out onto a countertop dusted with additional powdered sugar and roll out to ⅛-inch thick. Cut into heart shapes and dry thoroughly. Dip in melted chocolate. Store in refrigerator.

Honey Moon

1 cinnamon stick
5 cloves
1 piece bruised root ginger
Grated rind of 1 lemon
½ vanilla pod
2 crushed cardamom pods
1 pound honey (2 cups)

Method

Put the spices and lemon rind in a jar. Cover with the honey and leave in a dark cupboard for 3 weeks. Add some to the ritual cup or use to flavor food and drinks at the handfasting.

Violet Twilight

1 pound sugar (2⅔ cups)
7 ounces water (⅞ cup)
½ teaspoon cream of tartar
4 drops purple food coloring
½ teaspoon violet essence (or vanilla extract)
2 dozen crystallized violets (or fresh violet flowers used immediately)

Method

To make a fondant, place the sugar and water in a heavy pan. Stir over low heat until the sugar has dissolved. Turn up the heat and bring to a boil. Add the cream of tartar and continue boiling. Take temperature readings using a sugar thermometer until the mixture reaches 114°C or 240°F. Remove from heat and stir in the flavoring and food coloring. Allow the mixture to cool a little, then turn out onto the counter, which should first be dampened with cold water. Sprinkle cold water over the fondant and let stand for 4 minutes. Using a knife or spatula, work the mixture until it becomes smooth and opaque. Flatten the mixture with your hands or a rolling pin, and use small cookie cutters to cut out 24 pieces, or make small fondant balls with your hands and flatten them. Press a crystallized violet into each and allow to harden for 1 hour.

Freya's Delight
6 apples, cored
3 ounces dried mixed fruit, chopped (6 tablespoons)
½ tablespoon crushed hazelnuts
4 ounces hazelnuts, shelled and roughly chopped (½ cup)
2 tablespoons rolled oats
3 chopped apricots
½ pint cider (1 cup)

Method
Stand the apples in an ovenproof dish and fill with the other dried ingredients. Pour the cider around the bases of the apples and bake in a moderate oven at 325°F/170°C/gas mark 3 for 40 minutes, until the apples are cooked, basting every ten minutes.

Wines and Ales

Making Wine
Wine can be made out of anything that is edible, from turnips and oak leaves to hawthorn blossoms. The flavor and perfume is extracted from the original ingredients and yeast and sugar are added to turn it into alcohol. The process is actually quite simple and requires little specialist equipment. Looking around brewing shops you might think it requires a large investment in materials and chemicals—it doesn't.

Basic Equipment

You will need some basic equipment as follows:

1. A large plastic bucket or brewing bin for fermenting the pulp. You can buy purpose-made bins that have tightly fitting lids, but a plastic bucket well sealed with plastic wrap will serve exactly the same purpose.

2. A demi-jon or glass fermentation jar—the wine is left in this until fermentation has finished. Demi-jons can be obtained relatively cheaply from a number of outlets.

3. An airlock (the real thing)—this is partially filled with water and fitted on top of the demi-jon to allow the gasses produced from the fermentation process to escape from the jar and prevent bacteria from entering. For several years I made wine without using airlocks; I just sealed the top of the jar with plastic wrap or a plug of cotton wool. It is possible to do this, though the use of an airlock is advisable since they are inexpensive.

4. A muslin bag or material to strain the pulp. Muslin is closely woven and strains all the fibers from any pulp, though in the past I have used the knotted sleeve from an old shirt.

5. A siphon tube is a necessity; it allows you to remove your wine from the jar without disturbing any sediment. If you just try to pour wine from one large vessel to another, you might spill some, and we don't want that kind of wastage, do we?

6. You will also need bottles and corks for the finished product. Glass bottles are no problem; you will probably have several laying around. Make a habit out of washing and saving them. Unless your bottles have screw tops, you will need to buy new corks—old ones cannot be reused.

In addition you can buy a large variety of equipment including thermometers, filtering kits, hydrometers, bottle-corking machines, and so on. Personally, I have never found any of them necessary, but if your winemaking turns into a serious hobby, you might want to invest in them.

The Basic Steps of Winemaking

1. The ingredients (fruit, vegetables, flowers, etc.) are gathered and washed.

2. The equipment is thoroughly sterilized.

3. The fruit, flowers, etc., are placed in a brewing bin with water and some of the sugar.

4. After a day or two, the yeast is added and allowed to ferment on the pulp for a while.

5. The liquor is strained into a fermentation jar. Any remaining sugar is added and an airlock is fitted. The jar is put in a warm place to encourage fermentation.

6. When fermentation has finished after a few weeks (or sometimes months), the wine is "racked off," which means it is siphoned into a clean jar.

7. The wine is left to clear.

8. The wine is siphoned off into bottles. Most wines must be left to mature for several months before drinking.

The Yeast

It is now possible to buy a variety of yeasts developed for particular types of wines and beers. These will definitely give you a better result, though it is possible to use fresh or dried bread yeast. The main thing to remember about yeast is that it is a living ingredient and you need to keep it that way. It will not be active at low temperatures and will be killed by high temperatures. It is generally activated before being added to the other ingredients at around 21–22°C (about 65–70°F), which is just lukewarm. This method is employed in some of the recipes in this book.

A variety of beer yeasts are also available, which will enable you to brew mild, bitter, lager, stout, etc.

Yeast Nutrient

A nutrient is generally added at the same time as the yeast. This helps keep the yeast working and makes sure it converts more of the sugar to alcohol. You can make wine without it, but for a better fermentation and a stronger brew, it is best to use one. Old recipes call for the yeast to be floated on a piece of toast, which presumably served the same purpose. Yeast nutrients are available from specialist brewing shops and some drug stores (in the United Kingdom at least).

The Sugar

White refined sugar is generally used for winemaking. If you prefer, you can use brown sugar, though this will alter the taste of the wine.

Chemicals—To Use or Not to Use

A large variety of chemicals are available for use with wine and beer making. I try to avoid them whenever possible. After all, people have been making alcoholic beverages for millennia without them.

Acids

Wine needs a little acid to work. If none is present in the raw ingredients, it is necessary to add some, usually in one of two forms—citric acid or tannin.

Sometimes recipes call for tannin. This is present in the skins of some fruits and in tea; a cup of cold, black tea can be added in its place. It helps the wine to keep.

Citric acid is present in all citrus fruits, so instead of adding a teaspoon of citric acid, add the fresh juice of a lemon. It helps fermentation and improves the bouquet.

Pectic Enzyme

This is usually used in combination with fruits that contain a lot of pectin. If you make jam, you will know that pectin causes things to jellify. Pectic enzyme helps break down the pectin and get all the juice out of the fruit. Sometimes you might also have a wine that won't clear because of the high pectin content of the fruit, and pectic enzyme can be added to clarify the wine.

Sterilizing Tablets and Solutions

One of the most important things in wine and beer making is the cleanliness and thorough sterilization of the equipment. Bacteria can cause your must (fruit or vegetable pulp) to go moldy or later spoil the wine or turn it to vinegar.

In former times, sulphur fumes were used to sterilize the equipment and ingredients. These days, sterilizers generally come in the form of sodium metabisulphate, which gives off sulphur dioxide when combined with water. This can be used to clean equipment and added to the wine in the form of Campden tablets at the fermentation stage. It is possible to use boiling water to sterilize equipment, but I find the addition of a Campden tablet to some wines is necessary to kill off bacteria and prevent mold from forming. Some recommend the use of a Campden tablet each time the wine is transferred to a new vessel.

Wine from Fruit

Use good quality fruit and cut off any bad parts before washing thoroughly. If you have large fruits such as apples or pears, you will need to chop them. Put the fruit in a plastic bin and pour boiling water over it. Stir, cover, and leave to cool to lukewarm. Crush the fruit and add half the sugar, stirring to dissolve. Add the yeast and nutrient. Cover and let stand in a warm place for three days, stirring daily. Strain the liquor off the pulp into a demi-jon. Add the rest of the sugar and fit an airlock.

Wine from Flowers

Pick your flowers on a dry day and use them as quickly as possible. Remove any green parts and wash them gently but thoroughly. Flowers will need the addition of acids and nutrients, plus something like chopped raisins or grape concentrate to give the resulting wine any body. Put the yeast to ferment on the grape juice concentrate with the sugar in a brewing bin. When it is fermenting, add the flower heads and acids. Cover and let stand for seven days, stirring daily, pressing the flowers against the sides of the bin. Strain into a demi-jon and fit an airlock. Some people recommend putting the flowers in a muslin bag so they can be removed easily.

Wine from Vegetables

Wash the vegetables and cut off any bad parts. Chop them and simmer them in water until they are just softening. If you'd like, you can add some spices to the water. Strain them into a bin and add some citric acid, the sugar, and either chopped raisins or grape concentrate. When cool enough, add the yeast and nutrient. Cover and let stand in a warm place to ferment for three days. Strain into a demi-jon and fit an airlock.

Mead

Add water to the honey and bring to a boil, skimming off any scum. Add some cold black tea and, when cool enough, the yeast and nutrient. Pour into a demi-jon and fit an airlock.

Sparkling Wine

To make a sparkling wine, the wine must undergo a second fermentation. The wine is made in the usual way, but after racking, the wine is put in a cool place for six months to mature. Now more sugar must be added to begin a new fermentation at the rate of 2½ ounces per gallon. Take a little wine from the jar and dissolve the sugar in it before returning it to the demi-jon. Add some activated champagne yeast and wait for the process to start. This will take a few hours. The wine should then be siphoned into sterilized bottles with a gap of 2 inches at the top and fitted with wired corks. The bottles are then laid on their sides until the fermentation is complete. This will take a few days. The wine should then be stored on its side for 6–12 months before drinking. The stored wine bottles should be rotated regularly.

Brewing Beer

Beers are generally brewed from malt extract, sugar, hops, and yeast. There are various types of yeast to produce ale, bitter, stout, and lager. The malt extract is dissolved in warm water in the brewing bin. The hops are boiled for about 45 minutes, and the liquor is strained into the bin with the malt extract and sugar. When the liquid is cool enough, the started yeast is added and the bin covered and left to ferment in a warm place for 5–7 days. After this, the bin is removed to a cool place for a day or two, and then bottled. The beer usually improves after standing for 3–4 weeks.

Mead

4 pounds honey (8 cups)
Yeast and yeast nutrient, 1 sachet of each (available from brewing shops or specialty grocery stores)
1 orange
1 lemon
1 gallon water (16 cups)
Pectic enzyme

Method
Put the water and honey into a pan and bring to a boil. Allow to cool to 21°C (68°F). Add the juice of the orange and lemon, the yeast and yeast nutrient, and the pectic enzyme. (A yeast nutrient must be used as modern honey is deficient in important minerals.) Pour into a demi-jon and fit with an airlock. Allow to ferment and bottle (typically makes about 6 bottles). This should be matured for at least a

year in a cool dark place before drinking if you can possibly resist it that long!

Sweet Mead

4½ pounds honey (9 cups)
Juice of 2 lemons
Yeast and yeast nutrient, 1 sachet of each (available from brewing and specialty stores)
1 gallon water (16 cups)

Method

Boil half the water with the honey, stirring until the honey has dissolved. Remove from the heat. Allow to cool to 21°C (68°F) and add the lemon juice and nutrient. Add the rest of the water and transfer to a brewing jar. Add the yeast and fit with an airlock. When a layer of lees (sediment) settles at the bottom of the jar, rack off into a clean demi-jon. Keep for at least a year before drinking.

Handfasting Wine

1 gallon meadowsweet flowers (16 cups)
1 pound raisins, chopped (2 cups)
3 pounds white sugar (7 cups)
1 gallon water (16 cups)
1 cup brewed black tea
Yeast and yeast nutrient, 1 sachet of each (available at brewing and specialty stores)
Juice of 1 lemon

Method

Put the flowers, chopped raisins, and sugar in a brewing bin. Boil the water and pour over; stir to dissolve the sugar. Add the tea and lemon juice. Cool to 20°C (68°F) and add the yeast and yeast nutrient. Let stand in a warm place for 10 days, stirring twice a day. Strain into a demi-jon and fit with an airlock. Bottle when clear.

Bride Ale

2 pints water (4 cups)

1 3-inch piece ginger root

1½ pounds honey (3 cups)

Juice of 3 lemons

4 pints cold water (8 cups)

Yeast and yeast nutrient, 1 sachet of each (available at brewing and specialty stores)

Method

Boil the 2 pints (4 cups) of water with the ginger for 30 minutes. Meanwhile, put the honey into a brewing bin with the lemon juice and the cold water. Add the boiling water. Allow to cool to 20°C (68°F) and add the yeast and yeast nutrient. Cover and let stand for 24 hours in a warm place (65° or more). Strain and bottle. This can be drunk after seven days.

Mixed Drinks

Love Token

2 ounces sloe gin

1 egg white

½ teaspoon lemon juice

½ teaspoon raspberry juice

Method

Shake all the ingredients together well with crushed ice. Strain into a cocktail glass.

Lovers' Cup

1 bottle red wine

Juice of 1 orange

Juice of 1 lemon

6 whole cloves

3 sticks cinnamon

Brown sugar to taste

Method
Place the wine, fruit juice, and spices in a pan and bring slowly to a boil. Simmer gently 5–10 minutes. Remove from the heat and add the sugar to taste, stirring until dissolved. Serve warm.

Pledge of Love
1½ ounces peach brandy
1 tablespoon honey

Method
Stir well in a goblet.

Love Knot
1½ ounces blended whiskey
1 egg white
1 teaspoon lemon juice
½ teaspoon powdered sugar
¼ teaspoon anise

Method
Shake well with crushed ice. Strain into a cocktail glass.

Celebration Punch
1 pound sugar cubes (2 cups)
2 lemons, sliced
2 4-quart bottles lemonade
6 oranges, sliced
1 pint strawberries
4 1-quart bottles champagne or sparkling wine
1 1-quart bottle brandy
1 1-quart bottle sherry
1 1-quart bottle Madeira wine
4 ounces cherry brandy (½ cup)

Method
Rub the sugar cubes over the lemons until they have absorbed all the yellow part of the skins of 2 lemons. Mix the sugar, lemonade, and fruits in a punch bowl. Add the remaining ingredients and ice. Stir well.

Passion Punch
1 pint tea made with two tea bags (2 cups)
1 pint apple juice (2 cups)
1 pint ginger beer (2 cups)
4 tablespoons lemon juice

To decorate:
Lemon slices
Maraschino cherries

Method
Make the tea and remove the tea bags. Add the other liquids. Transfer to a punch bowl and decorate with the fruit.

Irish Coffee
1½ ounces Irish whiskey
1½ teaspoons sugar
Black coffee
Whipped cream

Method
Pour the whiskey into a coffee cup. Add the sugar and fill with hot black coffee. Stir to dissolve sugar. Float whipped cream on top; do not stir. Add a straw if desired.

Atholbrose
1 teaspoon clear honey
1 shot of whiskey

Method
Stir the honey into the whiskey and drink. Quantities can be adjusted to taste. In Scotland, this is considered an ideal breakfast drink!

Mulled Wine

½ pound brown sugar (1 cup)
½ pint water (1 cup)
1 lemon
1 orange
12 whole cloves
1 cinnamon stick
½ teaspoon ginger powder
2 ounces raisins (¼ cup)
2 bottles red wine

To decorate:
Orange and lemon slices

Method
Put the brown sugar and water in a pan and heat slowly to dissolve. Add the juices of the lemon and orange, their grated rinds, and the spices. Boil for 5 minutes. Remove from heat and allow to infuse for an hour. Strain into a large pan, add the raisins, and bring to a boil. Add the wine, but do not allow it to boil (all the alcohol disappears!); just warm it through over low heat. Serve hot in glasses decorated with orange and lemon slices.

Mulled Mead

1 pint mead (2 cups)
½ ounce bruised ginger (1 tablespoon)
4 cloves
1 cinnamon stick

Method
Heat the mead to no hotter than 60°C (140°F) with the bruised ginger, cloves, and cinnamon.

Plighting Cup

1 ounce coriander herb, ground (2 tablespoons)

1 pint boiling water (2 cups)

Method

Infuse for 15 minutes. Strain. Coriander is a powerful binding herb of love, celebrating both the sacred love of the Lord and Lady and the love of human couples.

Betrothal Cup

½ pint boiling water (1 cup)

2 teaspoons dry (or 1 tablespoon fresh) marjoram

Method

Infuse for 15 minutes. Strain. Marjoram is sacred to the Goddess of Love.

Chapter 11

SPELLS AND
LUCKY CHARMS

*M*arriage is one of life's great rites of passage. During the ceremony, the bride and groom are in a threshold state, neither married nor unmarried. This is a circumstance of potentially great magical power, which the guests were always keen to tap into, hence all the customs of taking pieces of the bride's dress, her flowers, and so on. However, while any threshold is powerful (whether it is a time that is not a time, a place that is not a place, a gateway, or a rite of passage), it is also very dangerous. When a person crosses a threshold, they are in danger from the spirits that dwell *between*. For this reason, a bride—in a liminal stage of life—is carried across the threshold into her new house. Also for this reason, much wedding magic is concerned with the protection of the bride and groom.

The character of the wedding is an act of sympathetic magic that sets the tone for the rest of the couple's life together. If it is surrounded by symbols of prosperity and plenty, then this is thought to attract these things later on.

Nordic Protection Pouch

1 pinch chives, dried
1 pinch rosemary, dried
1 garlic clove
1 iron nail
3 x 3-inch square of blue cloth
1 x 9-inch length of red thread

Based on a Swedish tradition, this pouch should be secreted about the groom's clothes to protect him from the attentions of jealous forces. It may be prepared by the groom or one of his friends, though not the bride. Take the cloth and sprinkle in the herbs and add the nail, concentrating on the thought of keeping the groom safe on his wedding day and beyond. "Project" this thought into the herbs, and tie up the pouch with the red thread.

Pre-Ceremony Purification Bath

Before the wedding ceremony, you might like to indulge in a purification bath to ensure that you are cleansed, body and soul, for what lies ahead.

2 handfuls salt
2 drops camomile oil (for calm and relaxation)
1 drop rosemary oil (for purification)
1 drop rose oil (for love)
1 drop lime oil (for energy)

Drop the oils into the salt and, using a pestle and mortar, blend the oils and salt together. You might like to add coloring, red for love or blue for purification, in the form of a drop of food coloring. Don't overdo this—you don't want to be blue for the ceremony, unless you are having a Pictish wedding complete with woad stains!

Love Locks

The couple should each cut a lock of the other's hair. These are placed in a wooden or silver box, which is then buried in the garden or some private site that is special to the pair. For as long as the box and hair endure, the lovers will be linked together.

Five Almonds

A gift of five almonds represents health, wealth, long life, fertility, and happiness.

Four Feohs

A Nordic tradition is to give the couple a gift of four feoh runes, in the form of a carving or painting, or maybe four feohs painted on four stones. They represent flax, fodder, fertility, and food.

Mehndi

In India and North Africa, the bride is adorned with henna patterns called *mehndi,* which are lucky and protect her from evil spirits. The painting is a great occasion shared by her female family members and friends.

If you want to decorate your bride, kits containing all you need are readily obtainable, or you can make your own using henna and a couple of other simple ingredients. Please remember to apply a "patch test" to make sure the skin is not sensitive to the ingredients.

Wash the area where you wish to apply the design and pat it dry. Mix the henna powder with water to the consistency of a pancake mix and let it stand for about 30 minutes. Rub a small amount of eucalyptus oil into the skin. You can use a stencil or squeeze applicator to apply the designs. Leave the henna in place for 10 minutes until the mixture is dry to the touch. Remove the stencil, if used. Gently brush lemon juice over the design. Wait another 30 minutes and apply more lemon juice. Freehand patterns may be formed by gradually building up the henna with several applications. As it dries, the henna will harden on the skin. The darkness and permanence of the design will depend on your skin type and color and how long the henna mixture is left in place. Leave in place for 3–24 hours, keeping the painted area of skin out of direct sunlight. Remove the hardened henna with water. As a rough guide, mehndi designs can last anywhere from a couple of days to several weeks.

Mehndi is usually trouble-free, but should not be applied to damaged skin, the face (especially near the eyes), or other sensitive areas. If you have allergies or sensitive skin, test the procedure on a small area before applying a large design. Avoid getting the henna on your hands, clothes, furnishings, or anywhere else where you don't want it to stain. If this does happen, wash it off immediately.

Rosemary Wedding Wreath

There is an old eastern European custom of the bride wearing a wreath or chaplet of rosemary, which symbolizes love and remembrance. The wreath is woven for the bride on the wedding eve by her friends, each making a wish for the bride as they attach a piece of rosemary to the chaplet (for instructions on making wreaths, see the section "The Bridal Wreath" in chapter 9). Each person might say one of the following, or add something of their own:

I wish the bride wisdom.

I wish the bride loyalty.

I wish the bride love.

I wish the bride happiness.

I wish the bride wealth.

I wish the bride health.

Yarrow Marriage Charm

On a Friday during the waxing moon, take nine dried yarrow flower heads, and bind the stems together. Add a green ribbon, tie it into a bow, and hang the posy over the bridal bed to ensure everlasting love.

Lucky Horseshoe

A lucky horseshoe is given to the bride and groom to keep in their home. English brides carry cardboard horseshoes on their wedding day.

The Bridal Bed

It is traditional for the bride's friends to prepare the bridal bed and bedroom for the wedding night. The Greeks think it proper to roll young babies over the bed as a fertility ceremony, while the Chinese encourage young children to sit on it for similar reasons. The bed may be strewn with flowers, seeds, fruits, and money, all to ensure fertility and prosperity on all levels. It might be a good idea to put the seeds and fruits in packets as they might be difficult to remove from the sheets. In Greece, young unmarried women also shower the bed with coins, flowers, and sugar-coated almond candies (koufetta).

Sicilian Pillow Charm

Two days before the wedding, the mother of the bride puts money under her daughter's pillowcase, and the mother of the groom puts money under her son's pillowcase in an act of sympathetic magic to ensure that they will always be prosperous. If you can't get the two mothers to do this, ask two older female members of the coven or two married friends.

Celtic Love Knot

This knot symbolizes the eternity of love, and Irish brides sometimes embroider it into the handkerchief that they will carry on the day of the wedding. If you want to make one, you can do it as a magical act, reinforcing your love with each embroidery stitch.

Best Man Spell

Based on a Russian custom, the best man can perform a protection spell for the bride by walking three times around her carrying the coven pentacle. The other members of the party shout and bang drums to frighten away negativity. He then kneels in front of her and scratches the ground before her with his athame, declaring that she is protected from anyone who may wish to harm her, human or spirit.

Floral Plenty Charm

Hide a little bread, salt, sugar, and a coin in the bouquet, or carry these in a small silk purse to ensure a life that will never want for food or money.

Lucky Break

Greek weddings are characterized by the enthusiastic breaking of plates, symbolizing luck.

Thirteen Coin Spell

The Spanish groom gives his bride thirteen golden coins to symbolize his ability to provide for her. The modern Pagan bride may well be the one to present this gift to the groom, but whichever way you do it, place the coins in a small pouch and hand them over at the conclusion of the ceremony. They are passed back and forth several times, but end up in the possession of the bride. You could even use chocolate coins in gold paper and eat them afterwards—the symbolism is the same.

Chapter 12

HANDPARTING

---

*E*ven with the best intentions in the world, relationships sometimes do not work out. The couple may simply go their separate ways, hopefully without recrimination or blame, or choose to undergo a formal handparting ceremony. One partner should not force the other into this, and it should only be done if both parties are on friendly enough terms to undertake it with good will, to bring closure to the relationship and allow each other to move on.

The Handparting Ritual

The candles and the altar should be black, which is the color of Saturn and the color of endings. One lit black candle, representing the ending relationship, is placed on the altar, flanked by two unlit blue candles for healing. The couple hold the ends of the cord with which they were originally bound for the duration of the ceremony, until it is cut by the celebrant. A very sharp knife or shears are placed on the altar for this purpose.

The celebrant casts the circle in the usual manner and announces:

> *We are here to mark the handparting of [name] and [name], who wish to separate from each other at this time.*

The celebrant then addresses the bride:

> [Name], have you come here of your own free will to seek handparting from [name]?

Bride: *I have.*

The celebrant then addresses the groom:

> [Name], have you come here of your own free will to seek handparting from [name]?

Groom: *I have.*

Celebrant: *Then let you be parted without recrimination or blame, neither seeking ill for the other. Remember that this has been one of life's lessons, and you have learned from your relationship. Cherish the memory of good times you have shared, and relinquish the pain. [Names of bride and groom], are you willing to do so?*

Bride: *I am.*

Groom: *I am.*

Celebrant: *I declare before the Lord and Lady and your brothers and sisters of the Craft that you are no longer handfast. [The celebrant cuts the cord they hold between them.] Let each of you take your own blue candle, which represents the healing journey each of you must now take. [They each light their separate candle from the black central candle, which is then extinguished as a sign that the relationship is finally over. The cords and this candle are burned in the fire, either now or later, by the celebrant.]*

The celebrant uses the incenses to cleanse the aura of each, saying:

> Forget painful thoughts and remember each other kindly.

The celebrant makes the sign of the pentacle before each with their blue candle, and says:

> Let anger and hatred burn away.

The celebrant sprinkles each with water, saying:

> *Be cleansed of heartache and regret.*

The celebrant places a few grains of salt in each of their palms, and says:

> *Return to the world and take up your life anew.*
>
> *The rite is ended. Go in peace.*

The handparted couple then walk to opposite quarters of the circle and exit in different directions.

POEMS AND BLESSINGS
FOR HANDFASTINGS

An Irish Blessing

May the flowers always line your path
And sunrise light your day,
May songbirds serenade you,
Every step along the way,
May a rainbow run beside you,
In a sky that's always blue,
And may happiness fill your heart,
Each day your whole life through.

Irish Toast

Friends and relatives, so fond and dear, 'tis our greatest pleasure to
have you here. When many years this day has passed, fondest mem-
ories will always last. So we drink a cup of Irish mead and ask God's
blessing in your hour of need.

The guests respond: *On this special day, our wish to you, the good-ness of the old, the best of the new. God bless you both who drink this mead, may it always fill your every need.*

Some Blessings Guests Might Like to Use

May your hearts be as warm as your hearthstone.

May God sleep on your pillow.

May God be with you and bless you.

May you see your children's children.

May you be poor in misfortune, rich in blessings.

May you know nothing but happiness from this day forward.

A generation of children on the children of your children.

Love Poetry

You might like to read one of these classic love poems as part of the ceremony, or at the reception, or adapt part of them for your vows.

Roisin Dubh (Little Black Rose)

Roisin, have no sorrow for all that has happened to you
The Friars are out on the brine, they are travelling the sea
Your pardon from the Pope will come, from Rome in the East
And we won't spare the Spanish wine for my Roisin Dubh

Far have we journeyed together, since days gone by.
I've crossed over mountains with her, and sailed the sea
I have cleared the Erne, though in spate, at a single leap
And like music of the strings all about me, my Roisin Dubh

You have driven me mad, fickle girl—may it do you no good!
My soul is in thrall, not just yesterday nor today
You have left me weary and weak in body and mind
O deceive not the one who loves you, my Roisin Dubh

I would walk in the dew beside you, or the bitter desert
In hopes I might have your affection, or part of your love
Fragrant small branch, you have given your word you love me
The choicest flower of Munster, my Roisin Dubh

If I had six horses, I would plough against the hill—
I'd make Roisin Dubh my Gospel in the middle of Mass—
I'd kiss the young girl who would grant me her maidenhead
And do deeds behind the lios with my Roisin Dubh!

The Erne will be strong in flood, the hills be torn
The ocean will be all red waves, the sky all blood,
Every mountain and bog in Ireland will shake
One day, before she shall perish, my Roisin Dubh.
  —15th/16th century Irish

No sickness worse than secret love
It's long, alas, since I pondered that
No more delay; I now confess
My secret love, so slight and slim

I gave a love that I can't conceal
To her hooded hair, her shy intent
Her narrow brows, her blue-green eyes
Her even teeth and aspect soft

I gave as well—and so declare—
My soul's love to her soft throat
Her lovely voice, delicious lips
Snowy bosom, pointed breast

And may not overlook, alas,
My cloud-hid love for her body bright
Her trim straight foot, her slender sole,
Her languid laugh, her timid hand

Allow there was never known before
Such a love as mine for her
There lives not, never did, nor will,
One who more gravely stole my love

Do not torment me, lady
Let our purposes agree
You are my spouse on this Fair Plain
So let us embrace
—Anonymous, 15th/16th century

Set that berry-colored mouth
On mine, O skin like foam
Place that smooth and lime-white limb
—despite your quarrel—round me

Slim and delicate, be no longer
Absent from my side
Slender, show me to your quilts!
Stretch our bodies side by side

As I have put away (soft thigh)
Ireland's women for your sake
Likewise try to put away
All other men for me

I gave to your bright teeth
Immeasurable longing
So it is just that you should give
Your love in the same measure.
—Anonymous

She is unique; there is no one like her.
She is more beautiful than any other.
Look, she is like a star goddess rising
At the beginning of a glorious new year;
Brilliantly white, clear skinned;
With beautiful eyes for looking,
With honeyed lips for speaking;
She says not one word too many.
With a long neck and white breast,
Her blue-black hair like lapis lazuli;
Her arm more dazzling than gold;
Her fingers like lotus flowers,
With heavy buttocks and tiny waist.
Her thighs offer her beauty,
As lightly she treads upon ground.
She has captured my heart in her embrace.
—Extract from a 3,000-year-old Egyptian papyrus

Sonnets from the Portuguese

How do I love thee? Let me count the ways.
I love thee to the depth and breadth and height
My soul can reach, when feeling out of sight
For the ends of Being and ideal Grace.
I love thee to the level of everyday's
Most quiet need, by sun and candle-light.
I love thee freely, as men strive for Right;
I love thee purely, as they turn from Praise.
I love thee with the passion put to use
In my old griefs, and with my childhood's faith.
I love thee with a love I seemed to lose
With my lost saints,—I love thee with the breath,
Smiles, tears, of all my life!—and, if God choose,
I shall but love thee better after death.

—Elizabeth Barrett Browning (1806–1861)

Sonnet 116

Let me not to the marriage of true minds
Admit impediments. Love is not love
Which alters when it alteration finds,
Or bends with the remover to remove.
Oh, no! it is an ever-fixed mark
That looks on tempests and is never shaken;
It is the star to every wandering bark,
Whose worth's unknown, although his height be taken.
Love is not Time's fool, though rosy lips and cheeks
Within his bending sickle's compass come;
Love alters not with his brief hours and weeks,
But bears it out even to the edge of doom.
If this be error and upon me proved,
I never writ, nor no man ever loved.
—William Shakespeare (1564–1616)

Of Pearls and Stars

The pearly treasures of the sea,
The lights that spatter heaven above,
More precious than these wonders are
My heart-of-hearts filled with your love.

The ocean's power, the heavenly sights
Cannot outweigh a love filled heart.
And sparkling stars or glowing pearls
Pale as love flashes, beams and darts.

So, little, youthful maiden come
Into my ample, feverish heart
For heaven and earth and sea and sky
Do melt as love has melt my heart.
—Heinrich Heine (1799–1856)

My True Love Has My Heart

My true-love hath my heart and I have his,
By just exchange one for the other given;
I hold his dear and mine he cannot miss;
There never was a better bargain driven.
My true-love hath my heart and I have his.

His heart in me keeps him and me in one;
My heart in him his thoughts and senses guides;
He loves my heart for once it was his own,
I cherish his because in me it bides.
My true-love hath my heart and I have his.
  —Philip Sidney (1554–1586)

Song: To Celia

Drink to me, only with thine eyes
And I will pledge with mine;
Or leave a kiss but in the cup,
And I'll not look for wine.
The thirst that from the soul doth rise
Doth ask a drink divine:
But might I of Jove's nectar sup
I would not change for thine.

I sent thee late a rosy wreath,
Not so much honoring thee
As giving it a hope that there
It could not withered be
But thou thereon didst only breathe
And sent'st it back to me:
Since, when it grows and smells, I swear,
Not of itself but thee.
  —Ben Jonson (1572–1637)

ANNIVERSARIES

Traditional Anniversary Gifts

First: Cotton. You could make your beloved a present of a new robe, altar cloth, or tarot bag.

Second: Paper. How about a good book on magic? Or a blank book for a Book of Shadows or Magical Diary? Tarot cards would also fall under the heading of "paper."

Third: Leather or straw. Leather might include a leather pouch for ritual equipment, or sandals for ritual use. If you go for straw, a handmade corn dolly would be appropriate.

Fourth: Flowers. Flowers are always acceptable, and you can be as extravagant as you like.

Fifth: Wood. Your lover might appreciate a box to hold ritual tools or tarot cards, an altar fashioned from an antique table or chest, or wood for a wand or staff.

Sixth: Iron or sugar. Sugar might mean cakes and a celebratory meal together. Iron, on the other hand, might refer to an athame (ritual knife) candlestick, cauldron, etc.

Seventh: Wool or copper. A woolen cloak might be appreciated for those cold winter rituals, or what about a nice copper pentacle for the altar? Copper jewelry and talismans would also be appropriate, especially as it is the metal of Venus.

Eighth: Bronze. A bronze statue of your lover's favorite god or goddess might be a nice anniversary gift.

Ninth: Pottery. This might include painted and decorated plates, a ritual cup, or small ceramic statuettes or candlesticks.

Tenth: Tin. This metal is associated with Jupiter, the planet of joviality and expansion. Perhaps you could make your beloved a talisman of Jupiter, or simply bring the influence of Jupiter into your lives by taking time to try new things and make new friends. Do something totally different for this anniversary to put some sparkle back into the relationship.

Eleventh: Steel. You needn't interpret this literally, but how about traveling in a steel vehicle, such as a car or train? You could visit a special place, such as a sacred site, together.

Twelfth: Silk and fine linen. This might be a silken robe or new cord handmade from silken threads.

Thirteenth: Lace. An altar cloth with lace edging would be a nice ritual present, or a special gift on a lace cushion could be fun.

Fourteenth: Ivory. Real ivory is not very environmentally friendly or ethical, so unless you can find an antique piece, stick to ivory-colored items. This could include flowers, clothing, pottery, or jewelry.

Fifteenth: Crystal. Crystals of all kinds would be suitable; maybe a healing crystal wand, a crystal pendant or earrings, a dowsing crystal, and so on.

Twentieth: China. This might include painted and decorated plates, a ritual cup, or small ceramic statuettes or candlesticks.

Twenty-Fifth: Silver. Silver jewelry, pentacles, or cloak pins are suitable, as is a silver chalice. Silver is also the color of the moon, so you might buy moon-shaped jewelry, plates, or linen with moon patterns.

Thirtieth: Pearl. This needn't mean pearl jewelry, but could be pearl-colored flowers or clothes or pottery with a pearlized glaze.

Thirty-Fifth: Coral. Again, coral is not very environmentally friendly or ethical, so unless you can find an old piece, stick to coral-colored items, or maybe go with a sea theme? Both are sacred to the Goddess of Love, after all.

Fortieth: Ruby. You might give your beloved jewelry, cuff links, or a tie pin with a real ruby, or go with a ruby-colored theme and buy ruby-colored goblets, flowers, or clothes.

Forty-Fifth: Sapphire. Again, you could buy something with real sapphires, or go with sapphire-colored flowers, glassware, pottery, etc.

Fiftieth: Golden. This is the metal of the sun and of the Sun God. Use it to bring some of his vital energy into your lives with gifts of gold rings or chains, or simply sun symbols, mobiles, and hangings.

Fifty-Fifth: Emerald. If you don't want to buy real emeralds, how about a trip to somewhere green, like the Emerald Isle (Ireland)? Or buy something eco-friendly that helps the environment.

Sixtieth: Diamond. The diamond is reputedly made from the flames of love, and sixty years together means that your love must be very strong and enduring. This anniversary could be the occasion of a family celebration, or you might like to spend it alone together over a quiet dinner. A diamond ring or pin would be a lovely gift.

HANDFASTING CERTIFICATES

Handfasting certificates are a recent innovation and a nice reminder of the day. Some high priest/esses will supply these, or you could design one on the computer or pen your own if you are good at calligraphy.

Certificate of Handfasting

Between . . . .

And . . . .

On this day [date] . . . .

Performed by . . . .

At [venue] . . . .

In the presence of these witnesses [signatures] . . . .

. . . .

. . . .

Attested by the celebrant [signature] . . . .

Appendix 4

HANDFASTING
INVITATIONS

Handfasting

You are invited to the handfasting of

.... and ....

On ....

At ....

Please wear ....

And bring ....

....

RSVP

Appendix 5

USEFUL ADDRESSES

The Pagan Federation
    BM Box 7097
    London
    WC1N 3XX
    United Kingdom
    www.paganfed.org

The Druid Order
    23 Thornsett Road
    London
    SE20 7XB
    United Kingdom

Association of Hedgewitches
    70 The Walmonds
    Tiverton
    Devon
    EX16 5EE
    United Kingdom

Children of Artemis

BM Artemis

London

WC1N 3XX

United Kingdom

www.witchcraft.org

Fellowship of Isis

Clonegal Castle

Enniscorthy

Eire

www.fellowshipofisis.com

LifeRites (provides list of celebrants willing to officiate)

P.O. Box 101

Aldershot

GU11 3UN

United Kingdom

Odinshof

BCM Tercel

London

WC1N 3XX

United Kingdom

Order of Bards, Ovates and Druids

P.O. Box 1333

Lewes

East Sussex

BM7 7ZG

United Kingdom

druidry.org

Pagan Alliance, Inc.
P.O. Box 666
Williamstown
VIC 3016
Australia

Ar nDraiocht Fein (American Druid Order)
P.O. Box 516
E. Syracuse, NY
13057
USA

International Gay and Lesbian Pagan Coalition
P.O. Box 26442
Oklahoma City, OK
73126-0442
USA

Nordic Pagan Federation
P.O. Box 1814
Bergen
Norway
www.eutopia.no/Nordic.htm

Sacri Radici
Co 54 Forli Centro
47100 Forli
Italy

The Witches' Voice
P.O. Box 4924
Clearwater, FL
33758-4924
USA
www.witchvox.com

Index

To Write to the Author

If you wish to contact the author or would like more information about this book, please write to the author in care of Llewellyn Worldwide and we will forward your request. Both the author and publisher appreciate hearing from you and learning of your enjoyment of this book and how it has helped you. Llewellyn Worldwide cannot guarantee that every letter written to the author can be answered, but all will be forwarded. Please write to:

Anna Franklin
℅ Llewellyn Worldwide
P.O. Box 64383, Dept. 0-7387-0668-X
St. Paul, MN 55164-0383, U.S.A.

Please enclose a self-addressed stamped envelope for reply,
or $1.00 to cover costs. If outside U.S.A., enclose
international postal reply coupon.

Many of Llewellyn's authors have websites with additional information and resources. For more information, please visit our website at http://www.llewellyn.com